A Content Analysis of the Three Television Networks

TV News Covers the Budget Debate

With a Foreword by Patrick D. Maines

Media Research Series

the media institute

Washington, D.C.

TV News Covers the Budget Debate

Copyright © 1986 The Media Institute

All rights reserved. No part of this publication may be reproduced or transmitted in any form without permission in writing from the publisher.

First printing January 1986.

Published by The Media Institute, Washington, D.C.

Printed in the United States of America.

ISBN: 0-937790-31-1

Library of Congress Catalog Card Number: 85-63319

Table of Contents

	Page
Foreword	v
Executive Summary and Conclusions	vii
I. Scope and Methodology of the Study	1
II. Social Security Cost-of-Living Allowance	7
III. Defense Spending	23
IV. Survey Research	39
V. Other Findings	47
VI. Appendix	55

Foreword

For many months now, one of the biggest economic stories in the country has been the efforts of the Congress and Administration to put together some kind of deficit-reduction package. Among the several proposals put forward, the two most contentious program areas in all of them have been defense and Social Security.

Thus it was that The Media Institute decided some time ago to look at the coverage of these issues by the three broadcast networks.

From the outset we were interested in two things. First, we wanted to know with what degree of comprehensiveness the networks as a whole were covering these complex issues. Second, we were interested in any <u>differences</u> among the three networks' coverage.

As often happens, the methodology we employed allowed us to make other observations as well, which now bulk large in the following report.

As shown in the Executive Summary, we come to two major conclusions. Network coverage was woefully lacking in comprehensiveness, and it was also woefully imbalanced.

Concerning the issue of comprehensiveness, we can well appreciate the fact that most people have access to more substantial news sources than the nightly news. On the other hand, prominent studies have indicated that people rely more on the broadcast networks than all other news outlets.

With respect to the obvious imbalance in the networks' coverage of defense spending and Social Security, we can anticipate a defense of this coverage issuing from the preferences of the people as a whole. It seems clear by our own audience survey that an overwhelming majority of U.S. citizens do not want to see a freeze put on Social Security COLAs, and it seems clear enough that there is no great public appetite for increased defense spending.

Still, if this is a defense of imbalance in media coverage it is a novel defense. The broadcast networks like to posture as fearless and objective chroniclers of the world's affairs--not as the sentinels of the opinions of a simple majority.

In his book <u>Amusing Ourselves to Death</u>, Neil Postman, a professor of communications at New York University, laments the shallowness of television news. "Under the influence of the printing press," he says, "discourse was different-- coherent, serious, and rational. Now under television it has become shriveled and absurd."

The inescapable conclusion of this study-- whether it comes as a surprise to anybody or not--is that Postman is correct.

Many of us may be familiar by now with the 30- and 60-second spots called "Amercian Television and You" currently being run as a "public service" by ABC. We would like to suggest that future spots contain a warning to TV viewers that what they see is an imbalanced and superficial presentation, with a recommendation that viewers consult their libraries or better newspapers for the rest of the story.

Now that would be a public service.

Patrick D. Maines
President
The Media Institute
November 1985

Executive Summary and Conclusions

The first year of President Reagan's second term began as the year of tax reform. As the spring of 1985 turned into summer, however, the Administration's much-heralded plan for simplifying the system of tax rates and deductions found itself stalled in the mire of special-interest politics, where it would languish through the fall.

Another, and perhaps more urgent, economic issue came quickly to the fore, grabbing the attention of both government officials and journalists. This was the growing federal deficit, and the budget debate that ensued (and in fact continues at this writing) in an attempt to stanch the flow of red ink.

As the battle of the budget was joined, The Media Institute decided to conduct a study of the television coverage it received, to ascertain the nature of budget coverage reaching the public through this popular news medium.

The battle was actually a collection of skirmishes taking place on several fronts. Therefore, the Institute decided to focus on two key areas: the Social Security cost-of-living allowance (COLA) and defense spending. These emerged quickly as two of the most politically charged as well as economically significant topics of debate.

Using a research technique known as content analysis, researchers analyzed all stories mentioning proposed COLA and defense cuts which appeared on the nightly evening newscasts of ABC,

CBS, and NBC during March, April, and May of 1985. The database comprised 56 stories.

Researchers analyzed the coverage to determine its comprehensiveness and balance. A story was considered adequately comprehensive if it reported the provisions of the proposal at hand, mentioned at least one effect the proposal might have, and explained any specialized terms. Balance was determined by measuring the amount of coverage given opposing viewpoints.

In addition to the content analysis, the Institute conducted a public-opinion poll of 798 respondents to determine their views on COLAs and defense spending, and how they felt the networks covered those issues.

FINDINGS

Several key findings emerged regarding network coverage of Social Security COLAs and defense spending:

* Over half of all network stories were not adequately comprehensive: 56.4 percent of Social Security and 65.2 percent of defense stories failed to meet even minimal criteria.

* Network coverage was overwhelmingly opposed to freezing the Social Security COLA: 66.9 percent of issues coverage opposed a COLA freeze, 23.9 percent favored a freeze, and 9.2 percent was neutral.

* Network coverage was overwhelmingly opposed to increases in defense spending: 65.5 percent of the issues coverage opposed increased spending, 31.1 percent favored increases, and 3.4 percent was neutral.

* Journalists were the single most frequently used sources of information for Social Security

(31.6 percent) and defense (27.0 percent). However, various categories of government officials, when taken collectively, were the sources of half of Social Security (49.5 percent) and almost two-thirds of defense stories (63.5 percent).

In summary, the networks offered comprehensive coverage of the COLA and defense-spending debates less than half of the time. In addition, coverage was clearly imbalanced: It opposed freezing COLAs and it opposed increased defense spending, in both cases by margins of two to one. Over four-fifths of the coverage relied on journalists and government officials as sources of information.

CONCLUSIONS

It seems apparent from the above findings that the three television networks, taken as a whole, were remiss in presenting the public with a comprehensive picture of the debate over Social Security COLAs and defense spending.

The test by which we judged comprehensiveness was admittedly arbitrary--but by no means stringent. Indeed, we asked only that a story report the provisions of a proposal, mention at least one possible effect or outcome of the provision, and explain complex or unclear budgetary terms. And yet over half of all stories could not meet these minimal criteria for what we called "adequate comprehensiveness."

One must wonder whether it is worth the time and effort of the networks to broadcast stories which do not meet even such simple measures as these. What kind of information is being conveyed? What can the viewer learn from such stories? Why bother watching?

This study's findings on the balance of coverage are no more encouraging. Viewers can hardly be expected to make an objective assessment of a public-policy issue when two-thirds of the news coverage favors a particular point of view. And yet this was the case in both the Social Security and defense coverage. Two-thirds of the Social Security coverage opposed a freeze on COLAs, just as two-thirds of defense coverage opposed increases in defense spending.

One can only speculate on why the networks reflected these particular views, and by such similar margins. We could invoke the theory of news media-as-government-adversaries, since the networks' positions on both issues contrast with the Administration's positions; or perhaps the networks are reflecting a popular sentiment that is abroad in the land; or perhaps, as many have argued, the networks are showing greater sympathy toward "liberal" points of view.

We are not sure what the reason is, or whether it really matters. What strikes us as important is that, for whatever reason, viewers were subjected to coverage which was not even remotely balanced.

Our conclusions thus far, that the coverage we studied was sadly lacking in comprehensiveness and woefully imbalanced, lead us to a third conclusion: A viewer relying primarily on network evening news coverage would have extreme difficulty in developing informed and objective judgments regarding budget initiatives on Social Security COLAs and defense spending.

At a time when the broadcast networks are losing audience share, it seems unlikely that they will move away from the sensationalism and superficiality that have characterized their news programs, especially in recent years. Nor are they likely to abandon the entertainment values that have come to shape their news productions. Thus, the prospects for better network news coverage appear dim, at least for now.

This is unfortunate, for as we must finally conclude, the coverage of COLAs and defense spending we analyzed can hardly be considered a service either to the individual viewer or to the larger cause of a well-informed public.

I. Scope and Methodology of the Study

The annual federal budget deficit hovers close to the $200-billion mark, and threatens to reach $250 billion by 1988 unless significant cuts are made. Many feel that these huge deficits are the most crucial economic problem facing this country, and that unless the spiraling deficits are brought under control, they will seriously endanger the continued growth and stability of the economy.

The daunting task of eliminating budget deficits of $200 billion or more per year has required the Reagan Administration and Congress to wrestle with some very tough choices on a wide variety of issues. The two most widely publicized, hotly debated, and politically potent of these have been the Social Security cost-of-living allowance, or COLA (a program that allows Social Security benefits to keep pace with annual inflation by automatically boosting benefits to coincide with the inflation rate), and defense spending.

These two issues significantly dominated the debate over, and coverage of, legislation proposed to lower the federal budget deficit. Since numerous studies show that the majority of people rely on television as their primary source of news, it is important to assess how these issues were reported by television, and what kind of impact the nature of television coverage might have on viewers' perceptions of the budget debate. Thus, this study examined network news coverage of the budget-reduction initiatives regarding Social

Security cost-of-living allowances and defense spending, using an analytical technique known as content analysis.

CONTENT ANALYSIS. Briefly stated, content analysis is an objective and reliable media-research technique for organizing communication content into various categories, and analyzing it through the use of a variety of statistical measures.

Researchers employed this technique to analyze television stories relating to two specific and significant aspects of the federal budget: Social Security cost-of-living allowances and defense spending.

Database. The database for the study comprised the nightly newscasts of ABC, CBS, and NBC during March, April, and May of 1985. Researchers analyzed all stories on the federal budget during this time period which specifically mentioned budget-reduction initiatives in Social Security cost-of-living allowances and defense spending. This time frame was selected because it was during these three months that the various proposals to reduce the deficit came to the forefront of debate between Congress and the Reagan Administration, and thus the proposals received heightened coverage.

Researchers used Vanderbilt University's Television News Index and Abstracts to identify stories dealing with the two topics during the selected time frames. Once the specific stories were chosen, the Vanderbilt Television News Archive compiled them on videocassette tapes which were rented to The Media Institute. To facilitate the coding process and to make more accurate determinations of the quantity of coverage, the tapes were then transcribed verbatim by an outside service. (It is extremely difficult for researchers to synchronize beginning and ending times when coding a category. Being off by only a second or two can make significant differences when analyzing television stories that may be only 10 to 20 seconds in length. Thus, researchers used the number of lines of coverage, rather than seconds, to give more accurate measurements of absolute and relative amounts of coverage.)

The database included a total of 56 actual television stories during the three-month period: 21 on ABC, 19 on CBS, and 16 on NBC. However, many individual stories reported on both Social Security and defense spending, which necessitated that they be coded as two separate stories--a Social Security story and a defense-spending story. Thus, for the purposes of this study, the database included 39 Social Security and 46 defense stories during the three-month period, for a total of 85 stories. By individual network, ABC, CBS, and NBC had 33, 31, and 21 stories respectively. (For the number of stories each network devoted to Social Security and defense spending, see Table 1.)

Table 1.
NUMBER OF SOCIAL SECURITY AND DEFENSE STORIES BY NETWORK

	SOCIAL SECURITY	DEFENSE	TOTAL
ABC	15	18	33
CBS	16	15	31
NBC	8	13	21
	39	46	85

Procedure. A pair of specially trained coders analyzed the selected stories, with inter-coder reliability checks conducted throughout to ensure agreement and accuracy.

The study was designed to yield measurements on "comprehensiveness" of the coverage of budget-reduction initiatives. Comprehensiveness is defined as (1) covering a matter under consideration completely or nearly completely so as to aid understanding of that matter; or (2) reporting or accounting for all or virtually all pertinent considerations related to a topic. In this study these considerations included the provisions, effects, and explanations of unclear budgetary terms related to the budget-reduction proposals.

For this study, these terms were defined as follows:

1. "Provision"--a written, formal statement of a condition; a stipulation or qualification; a portion of a Congressional bill or act; or a requisite action upon which rests the effectiveness of a proposal.

2. "Effect"--a discernible impact or change that would result if a particular proposal were implemented/not implemented; a resultant condition of a proposal. Effects were divided into four categories: (1) on the Budget/Budget Deficit; (2) on the Economy; (3) on Individuals; and (4) on Defense Programs/Defense of the Nation.

3. "Unclear Budgetary Terms"--words and terms associated with the budget that require further explanation before the uninitiated, or average, viewer can fully understand their meaning.

Thus, by the definition of comprehensiveness given above, coverage that included reporting on the provisions and effects surrounding a proposal, as well as defining or explaining unfamiliar words and terms related to the budget, would be considered "comprehensive." Coverage that consistently omitted any of these considerations would be considered "not comprehensive."

Researchers measured comprehensiveness by evaluating the amount of coverage (in lines) spent discussing the provisions and effects of the budget proposals, and by studying how frequently budgetary terms with complex or unclear meanings were defined in the budget coverage.

Although this study was originally executed to evaluate the comprehensiveness of network coverage of an important and topical issue, it allowed observations about the "balance" of coverage as well. Balance was determined by analyzing the diversity and symmetry of conflicting viewpoints. In other words, coverage that gave comparable weight to opposing perspectives would be considered "balanced," while coverage that focused predominantly on a single interpretation or viewpoint would be considered "imbalanced."

To measure the balance of coverage on Social Security COLAs and defense spending, researchers measured the amount of coverage (in lines) given to issues in support of and in opposition to a particular position, and then compared them. For this study, an "issue" was defined as a point of discussion, debate, or dispute surrounding the various budget proposals; or as a principle involved in discussions which involved value judgments. (For a complete list of the provisions, effects, issues, and unfamiliar words and terms related to the budget proposals, see Appendix.)

II. Social Security Cost-of-Living Allowance

With more than 36 million beneficiaries, Social Security is by far the largest entitlement program. The cost of Social Security and other federal entitlement programs, in FY 1985 alone, was approximately $425 billion--more than one-half of all federal revenues. Included in this total, according to an estimate by the Business Roundtable, is $67 billion which can be attributed to the cumulative effect of cost-of-living allowances (COLAs) authorized over the past five years to current recipients of Social Security and other federal retirement programs.

The debate over Social Security spending has centered around cost-of-living allowances. First authorized by Congress in 1972, COLAs have become an economic--and political--fixture. Cutting back on COLAs becomes extremely difficult for politicians, because senior citizens represent a strong, active voting bloc. Seniors are well represented by their own special-interest organizations, such as the American Association of Retired Persons (AARP) and the National Council of Senior Citizens. As the main beneficiaries of Social Security COLAs, senior citizens are adamantly opposed to any reductions in COLA benefits.

COMPREHENSIVENESS

Ideally, for network news viewers to be informed adequately about the Social Security proposals under consideration by Congress and the Reagan Administration, the networks should report all aspects surrounding a particular proposal. To be thoroughly comprehensive, this would necessitate covering the provisions of the proposal, the effects the proposal might have if enacted (e.g. on the deficit, economy, and/or individuals), and the viewpoints involved on both sides of the debate--points which both support and oppose freezing the COLA.

However, the networks choose not to provide in-depth and thoroughly comprehensive coverage; the 22-minute newscast is comprised of individual stories with an average length of 2-1/2 minutes. Television news coverage as it is practiced today does not lend itself to reporting complex issues in a comprehensive manner.

BY STORY. Instead of evaluating comprehensiveness by standards television rarely, if ever, meets, researchers proposed minimum criteria for the networks to meet to be considered adequately comprehensive. For instance, an "adequately comprehensive" story should define or explain all complex or unclear terms related to the budget, report the basic provisions of the proposal being covered, and mention at least one effect the proposal might have if enacted. This particular minimum standard for comprehensiveness allows the networks to relay all the information mentioned above in one sentence. For example: "The Senate budget proposal would freeze the cost-of-living allowance next year, cutting the budget deficit by $22 billion."

To better understand how this minimum standard was used to evaluate comprehensiveness of coverage, examples of different degrees of comprehensiveness are described below:

Adequately Comprehensive

"The (new budget compromise between Senate

Republican leaders and the White House) cuts back the expected 4-percent inflationary cost-of-living increase to 2 percent which works out for the average beneficiary to a cut of $81 in fiscal year '86, $198 in '87 and $314 in '88, cutting some $22 billon overall for the three years."

--ABC 4/5/85

Partially Comprehensive

"What follows now will be battle after battle and vote after vote to change the President's approved budget that puts a 2-percent cap on cost-of-living increases for Social Security recipients, and deep cuts, and in some cases outright elimination, of popular domestic programs."

--CBS 4/30/85

Not Comprehensive

"Appearing on NBC's Meet the Press, (former Vice President) Mondale said Mr. Reagan's agreement with Senate Republican leaders to cut back on the Social Security cost-of-living allowance contradicts the commitment he made during the election campaign."

--ABC 4/7/85

The first example was considered "adequately comprehensive" because the one unclear term, "cost-of-living increase," was explained as a "4-percent inflationary" measure, the provision of the proposal was given, and at least one effect the proposal might have if enacted was reported. In contrast, the second example was considered "partially comprehensive" because, although it gave a provision, it failed to report any effect should the proposal be passed into law. The third statement was considered "not comprehensive" since it failed to supply the viewer with either the proposal's provision or effect. Although it states that the proposal would "cut back on the Social Security" COLA, it is unclear what is meant by "cut back" (i.e. freeze the COLA? limit it to 1 percent? 2 percent? 3 percent?), and thus cannot be considered a provision.

When this minimum standard was used, as Chart 1 demonstrates, only 17 of the networks' 39 stories on Social Security (43.6 percent) were adequately comprehensive. In other words, over one-half of the stories failed to report the most basic information necessary to understand a proposal.

In assessing the performance of the individual networks, 53.3 percent of ABC's, 31.3 percent of CBS's, and 50.0 percent of NBC's stories were adequately comprehensive. Chart 1 shows that CBS had the fewest comprehensive stories, while ABC had the most, although all three networks did a

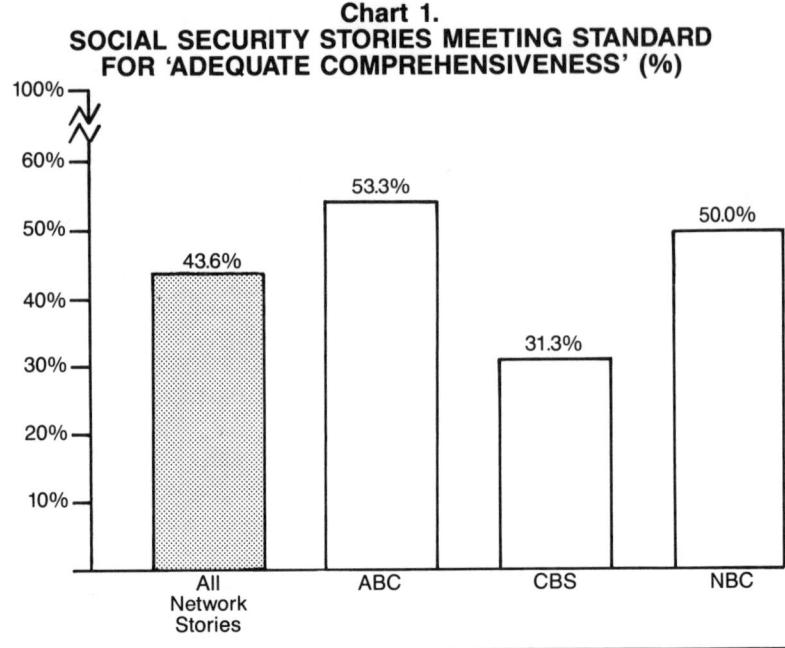

Chart 1.
SOCIAL SECURITY STORIES MEETING STANDARD FOR 'ADEQUATE COMPREHENSIVENESS' (%)

poor job overall in reporting comprehensive stories.

Another way to assess comprehensiveness by story is to simply tabulate the number of stories that report the most basic information of a proposal-- its provision(s). Of the 39 stories addressing Social Security, Chart 2 illustrates that nine (23.1 percent) completely neglected to report any provision of the proposal being covered, or else used undefined or unexplained terms which would likely render the provision unclear to the average viewer. Of the individual networks, NBC had only one of eight stories (12.5 percent) that failed to or did not adequately cover the provisions, while ABC reported four of 15 (26.7 percent), and CBS four of 16 (25 percent).

OVERALL COVERAGE. Because of the time restrictions of a 22-minute news show, many important stories are omitted, while others that do make the

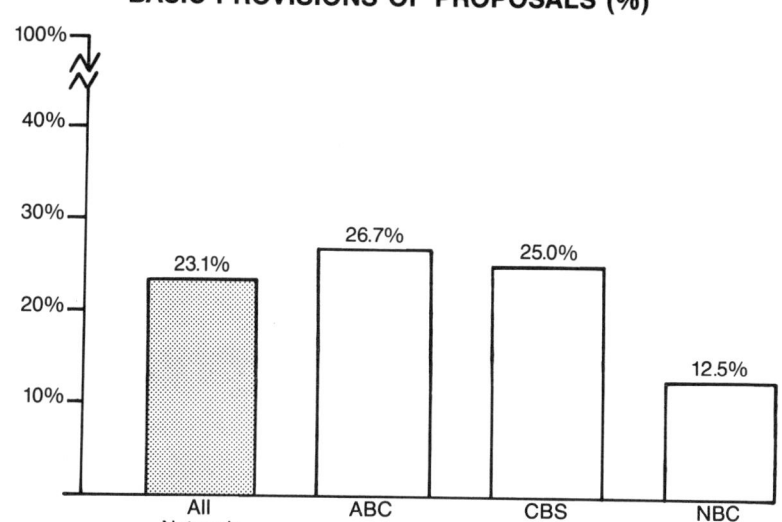

Chart 2.
SOCIAL SECURITY STORIES FAILING TO REPORT BASIC PROVISIONS OF PROPOSALS (%)

air are often compressed to the point where comprehension is sacrificed. Although critics have frequently taken the networks to task for the lack of comprehensiveness in news coverage, complaints have been dismissed with the response that the nightly newscast is, by its very nature, little more than a headline service. After all, some individual stories are only 10 to 20 seconds in length. Thus, researchers decided to evaluate the comprehensiveness of network coverage during the overall period of coverage. They surmised that while it may be difficult for the networks to do a comprehensive job of reporting a proposal in 30 seconds, the viewer should be fairly well-informed on all aspects surrounding a particular proposal over a three-month period. Unfortunately, even when comprehensiveness was evaluated in terms of overall coverage during the three-month period, network coverage* was sadly lacking.

Effects.

To assess comprehensiveness, researchers identified the various effects the Social Security proposals could have, if enacted, by closely monitoring Congressional hearings and print coverage, and keeping a list of all effects mentioned. Once the effects were identified, they were categorized as follows:

On the Budget/Budget Deficit.

Discussion of:

1. the amount by which a proposal would reduce

---

*Unless otherwise noted, all references to "network coverage" refer to the averages of data for ABC, CBS, and NBC. Data were collected for each network, but were averaged to discuss network coverage as a whole.

the deficit in FY 1986 or over a three-year period; of how much money a proposal would save;

2. a proposal's effect on other domestic programs in the budget;

3. a proposal as cutting the deficit far less than is necessary;

4. cuts as having no real impact; of "phantom" cuts from "unspecified" reforms;

5. the House budget package as cutting the deficit by about the same amount of money as the Senate budget package.

On the Economy.

Discussion of a proposal's effect on:

6. interest rates;

7. inflation;

8. tax increases;

9. economic growth;

10. health of the economy.

On Individuals.

Discussion of:

11. a proposal's effect on people with incomes greater than the official poverty line;

12. a proposal's effect on the approximately 3.3 million poor households that would experience losses of benefits averaging $10 to $15 per month;

13. a proposal's effect on the average retired worker's or couple's benefits over three years;

14. a proposal's effect on the average recipient's benefits over the course of a lifetime;

15. a proposal's effect on the ability of the elderly to pay for energy, food, visits to the doctor, busfare, etc.;

16. a proposal's effect on Supplemental Security Income (SSI) benefits to individuals;

17. COLA freeze proposal's effect on the average citizen's benefits for one month or one year;

18. COLA freeze proposal as causing between 280,000 and 570,000 elderly people to drop below the poverty line;

19. the effect of a two-percentage-point cut in COLAs on the average recipient's benefits over three years;

20. the effect of a two-percentage-point cut in COLAs on the average recipient for one month.

Of the 20 identified effects that might occur if the COLAs were frozen, overall network coverage failed to mention seven--over one-third--and focused predominantly on five effects at the expense of the others.

What is perhaps more revealing than the number of effects omitted from the coverage, however, is the amount of coverage devoted to the different categories of effects. Social Security effects were divided into three categories: "On the Budget/Budget Deficit," "On the Economy," and "On Individuals."

Overall, the networks were far more interested in the effect of the various Social Security COLA proposals on the budget and the budget deficit. (An example of an effect that would fall into this category: "The Senate plan would reduce the deficit by $22 billion if enacted.") Of the 215 lines devoted to coverage of Social Security effects, 115--53.5 percent--focused on the effect of the proposals on the budget and deficit. (As stated previously, lines were used instead of seconds to give a more accurate measure of amount of coverage.) Of the five specific effects in this category, all were mentioned during the period of coverage, although the effect regarding the amount of money that the proposal would save was the most popular, receiving 26.5 percent (57 lines) of the coverage devoted to Social Security effects.

Of the three networks' coverage in the "budget/budget deficit" category, ABC's accounted for 74 of the 115 lines (64.4 percent), and raised all five effects. CBS accounted for 31 lines (27.0 percent) and mentioned four effects, while NBC had 10 of the 115 lines (8.7 percent) and raised two effects.

The category of effects the networks emphasized next was "On Individuals." Sixty lines, or 27.9 percent of the effects coverage, was devoted to this category, which was concerned with the various proposals' impact on individuals. (For instance: "A COLA freeze would cost the average citizen about $18 per month or $216 per year.") Of the 10 specific effects in this category, one-half were not raised. The two specific effects most frequently reported were the proposals' impact on pushing the elderly below the poverty line (20 lines, or 33.3 percent), and on the ability of the elderly to pay for energy, food, doctors' visits, busfare, etc. (19 lines, or 31.7 percent).

Of the individual networks, CBS's coverage of effects on individuals was the most comprehensive, with 31 of 60 lines (51.7 percent) and four effects raised. NBC was next with 23 lines (38.3

percent) and three effects reported, while ABC followed with six lines (10.0 percent) and two effects mentioned.

The category of effects that received the least amount of coverage by the networks overall was "On the Economy." (An example of an effect in this category: "If implemented, the proposal could result in lowered interest rates.") The networks did not appear to place much importance on this category, because they devoted only 40 of a possible 215 lines (18.6 percent) to it. Of the five specific effects that fell within this category, only the one regarding a proposal's effect on tax increases received significant coverage. Of the 40 lines devoted to economic effects, it received 32, or 80.0 percent of the coverage. Two others received no coverage.

Of the three networks, ABC's coverage was the most comprehensive in this category; it accounted for 27 of the 40 lines (67.5 percent) and mentioned three effects. CBS and NBC raised the effect on tax increases only, using 12 lines (30.0 percent) and one line (2.5 percent) respectively.

Terms Explained.

Another measure of comprehensive coverage is the number of economic and/or budgetary words and terms with complex or unclear meanings that are defined or explained. Words and terms with complex or unclear meanings are defined as terms that require further explanation before the uninitiated, or average, viewer can fully understand their meaning. One can argue that if no explanation is offered for a budgetary or economic term which is central to a particular story but not commonly understood (e.g. the difference between a "real" freeze and a "nominal" freeze), then the average viewer will have little more than a superficial grasp of the story's meaning, and therefore its significance. (A list of the identified terms can be found in the Appendix.)

Again, network coverage did not fare very well. During the viewing period, the words and terms identified by researchers in Social Security stories were used by the networks 48 times; Chart 3 shows that 15 terms, or 31.3 percent, were not explained or defined by the networks. Chart 3 also demonstrates that individually, CBS did the best job of explaining and defining unclear terms, leaving two of 18 unexplained (11.1 percent). ABC used 14 terms and left three unexplained (21.4 percent), while NBC left 10 of 16 terms unexplained (62.5 percent).

SUMMARY. In summary, examination of the networks' coverage of the Social Security COLAs demonstrates that coverage was not comprehensive, regardless of whether it was measured by individual stories or by coverage over the three-month viewing period. If judged on a story-by-story basis, less than one-half of the stories met the minimum standard

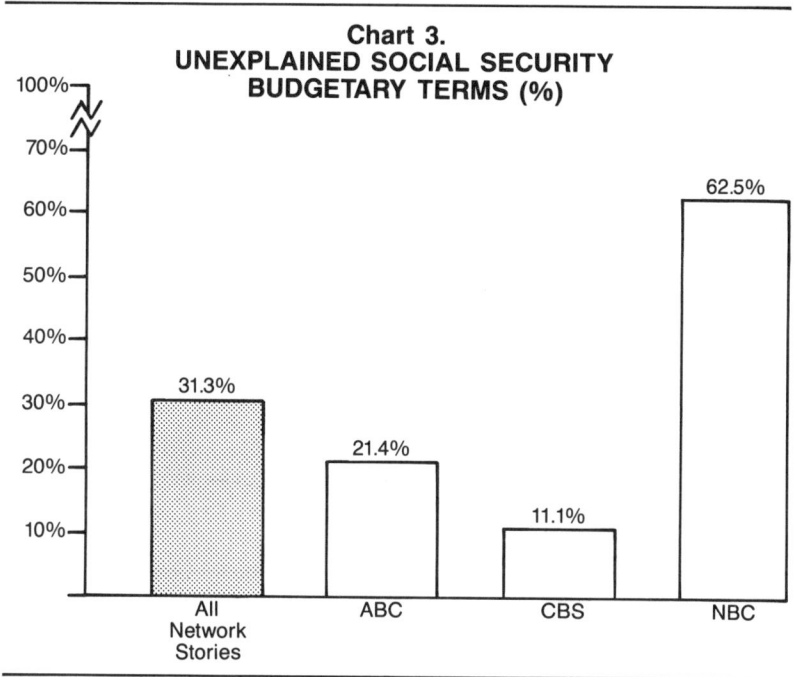

of comprehensiveness (as explained on page 8), and nearly one-fourth of the stories failed to give or explain adequately the basic provisions of the proposals. If judged by overall coverage, the networks did not fare much better. They consistently failed to report all of the most likely effects surrounding the proposals, and they neglected to explain or define unclear terms nearly one-third of the time.

Of the three networks, CBS devoted a larger portion of its coverage to Social Security than did the other two. CBS gave a total of 324 lines to coverage of Social Security issues, effects, and provisions, compared to 272 by ABC and 188 by NBC.

BALANCE

The COLA proposals proved to be useful measures of balance, because the issues surrounding them were markedly divided into two camps: issues in favor of and issues opposed to freezing the COLA. Researchers identified eight significant issues around which the Social Security debate centered. These were determined by analyzing all of the testimony presented in the Congressional hearings on the COLAs, as well as monitoring selected print-media coverage of the debate. In doing so, researchers found that these eight issues were repeatedly and consistently raised as the focal points of the Social Security budget debate. These issues, and the viewpoints they supported, are listed below:

Issues in Favor of Freezing the COLA:

1. Controlling the deficit is the top priority.
2. The elderly are fairly well-off.
3. The overall package of cuts spreads the effects over the majority of the population.

Issues Opposed to Freezing the COLA:

4. A freeze would result in the neglect of the poor and elderly.
5. The elderly are being asked to bear a disproportionate amount of cuts.
6. Social Security represents a contract/promise that cannot be broken.
7. Social Security adds nothing to the deficit.

Neutral Issues:

8. Larger issues of the Social Security system as a whole.

(Complete definitions of each issue can be found in the Appendix.)

To evaluate the balance of coverage on this controversial topic, researchers measured the amount of coverage (in lines) given to issues in support of and in opposition to freezing the COLAs.

Overall, network coverage was overwhelmingly opposed to freezing the COLA, by almost a three-to-one margin. As Chart 4 demonstrates, the networks devoted 277 lines, or 66.9 percent, to issues opposed to a COLA freeze. They devoted only 99 lines, or 23.9 percent, to issues supporting a COLA freeze. Neutral issues received 38 lines, or 9.2 percent of the issues coverage.

Chart 5 illustrates the amount of coverage provided for each individual issue. The majority of the coverage, by a wide margin, focused on the dispute over whether Social Security is an unbreakable contract or promise. For the most part, over one-half of the issues coverage—51.2 percent—centered on President Reagan's campaign promise not to touch Social Security. With the exception of the issue on the priority of controlling the deficit, which received 19.1 percent of the coverage, the remaining six issues each got less than 10 percent of the issues coverage.

Unsurprisingly, the three networks' individual

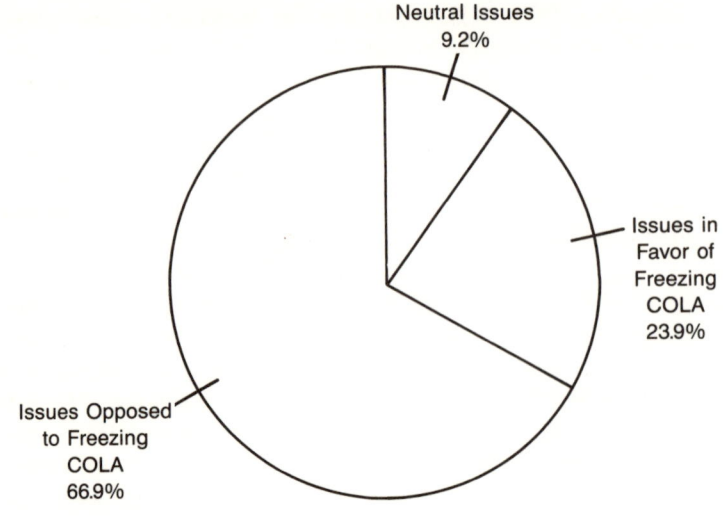

Chart 4.
COVERAGE DEVOTED TO ISSUES FAVORING AND OPPOSING COLA FREEZE (%)

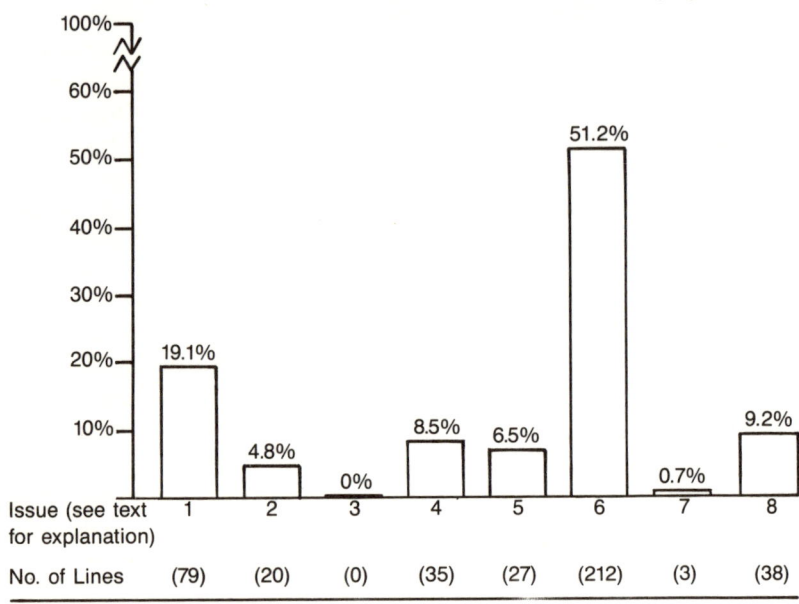

Chart 5.
SOCIAL SECURITY COVERAGE, BY ISSUE (%)

coverage of the COLA issues followed the overall network pattern. As Chart 6 shows, all three networks devoted more time to issues that opposed a COLA freeze. CBS presented the most balanced mix of opposing viewpoints, relatively speaking, although its coverage opposing a COLA freeze still predominated, 57.0 percent to 21.8 percent. Neutral issues received 21.2 percent of the CBS coverage. CBS also raised seven of the eight Social Security issues, and was the only network to address the larger issues of the Social Security system as a whole, and the debate over whether Social Security affected the federal deficit.

ABC's coverage opposed a COLA freeze, 69.6 percent to 30.4 percent. Of the eight Social Security issues, ABC raised only three, and was the only network that failed to report on the issues concerning the elderly: whether the elderly, as a group, are fairly well-off, or neglected. NBC's coverage was the least balanced of the

Chart 6.
COVERAGE DEVOTED TO ISSUES FAVORING AND OPPOSING COLA FREEZE, BY NETWORK (%)

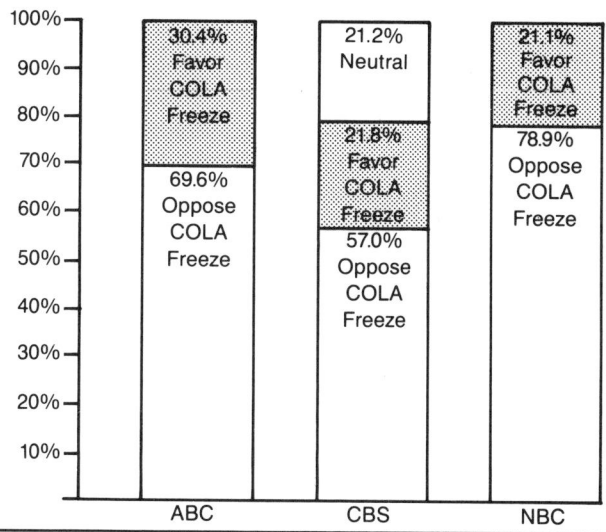

three, by a 78.9-percent to 21.1-percent margin, in opposition to a COLA freeze.

In summary, the coverage of the Social Security issues, both by individual network and overall coverage, was, in terms of viewpoints presented, overwhelmingly opposed to a COLA freeze, and thus markedly imbalanced.

CONCLUSION.

If the average viewer relied on television coverage as the sole source of information on the Social Security debate during the months of March, April, and May of 1985, he or she would not have had a very comprehensive understanding of the basic information regarding the different proposals. In addition, the average network viewer would have perceived the COLA debate as essentially a question of whether President Reagan broke his campaign promise on Social Security. While this might not be an insignificant issue in the COLA debate, the overwhelming emphasis on it represents an unquestionably limited perspective.

III. Defense Spending

The media have a penchant for what have been called "clear-cut" issues. These are issues that, above all, can be neatly divided into distinct sides.* The debate over whether to increase defense spending has been comprised mainly of these "clear-cut" issues. In part, the debate has been so divisive because, while some feel that the defense budget must bear the brunt of the budget cuts along with other programs (since one-fourth of all federal spending goes to defense programs), others claim that the defense budget requires special priority because reductions could adversely affect the security of the nation.

COMPREHENSIVENESS

As in the Social Security coverage, the networks chose not to report every aspect of defense-budget proposals, including all of the proposals' provisions and effects.

BY STORY. Taking this into account, researchers established a minimum standard to evaluate the comprehensiveness of network coverage of defense-spending proposals. To be "adequately comprehensive," a story must define or explain all

---
*Colin Seymour-Ure, The Political Impact of Mass Media (Beverly Hills, CA:Sage, 1974), p. 38.

complex or unclear terms related to the budget, report the basic provisions, and mention at least one effect the proposal might have if enacted.

To better understand how researchers applied this minimum standard, examples of different degrees of comprehensiveness are described below:

Adequately Comprehensive

"True, there is no tax increase in the Senate-passed budget, and it would save an estimated $56 billion next year, and nearly $300 billion over three years. But, Mr. Reagan's original request for a 6-percent defense-spending increase above inflation has been slashed to no money at all above the inflation rate for one year, and only 3 percent in the two years after."

--ABC 5/10/85

Partially Comprehensive

"(In the new GOP budget) defense spending would get zero growth. That is, it would only increase next year enough to cover inflation. It would run at 3 percent above inflation in the two years following."

--ABC 5/9/85

Not Comprehensive

"More fuel added to the federal budget fire storm. House Democrats and Republicans on the Budget Committee couldn't find the grounds for compromise, and tonight Democrats easily won a party-line vote for a budget that takes no cuts in Social Security increases, new deep cuts in defense-spending increases. A vote in the full

Democratic-controlled House now is expected the middle of next week."

--CBS 5/16/85

Researchers considered the first example "adequately comprehensive" because the provision and at least one effect of the proposal were given in clear and understandable terms. The second example, on the other hand, was considered "partially comprehensive" because it only gave the provision of the proposal, and failed to report on any effects it might have if passed into law. The third example was considered "not comprehensive" since it neglected to report either the proposal's provisions or effects. The reporter talks about "new deep cuts in defense-spending increases," but does not specify what those cuts are.

Network coverage of defense-spending proposals was even <u>less</u> comprehensive than COLA coverage.

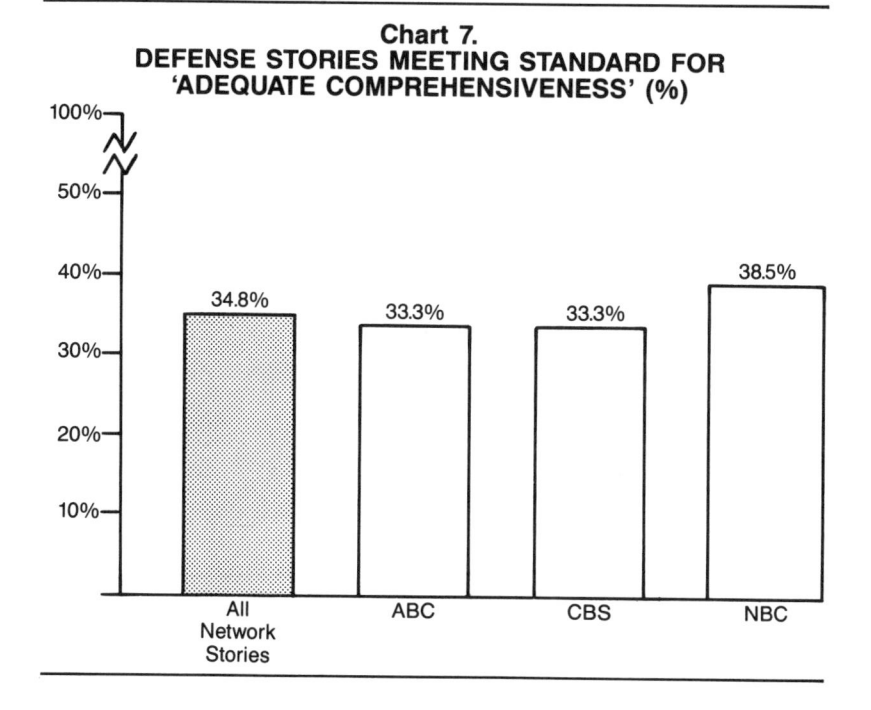

Chart 7.
DEFENSE STORIES MEETING STANDARD FOR 'ADEQUATE COMPREHENSIVENESS' (%)

	%
All Network Stories	34.8%
ABC	33.3%
CBS	33.3%
NBC	38.5%

Of the 46 stories that dealt with the defense budget, Chart 7 shows that 16 (34.8 percent) were adequately comprehensive. Thus, only about one-third of the defense stories reported the basic information needed to understand a proposal at more than a superficial level.

In evaluating the performance of the individual networks, researchers found the three about equally deficient in reporting adequately comprehensive stories. Of the stories on ABC and CBS, 33.3 percent were adequately comprehensive. NBC fared slightly better at 38.5 percent.

Comprehensiveness was also assessed by tabulating the number of stories that reported a proposal's provisions in understandable terms. As Chart 8 illustrates, over half of the stories on the defense budget (25 of 46) failed to report any provision of the proposal being covered. In this respect, coverage of the defense-spending proposals fared worse than coverage of the COLA pro-

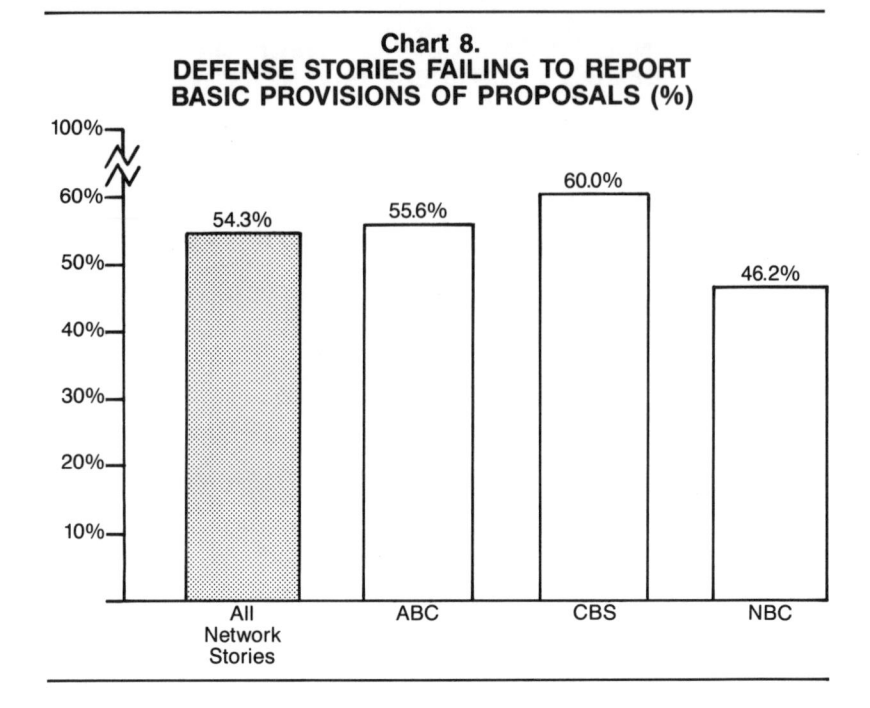

Chart 8.
DEFENSE STORIES FAILING TO REPORT BASIC PROVISIONS OF PROPOSALS (%)

Category	Percentage
All Network Stories	54.3%
ABC	55.6%
CBS	60.0%
NBC	46.2%

posals, where 23.1 percent of the Social Security stories neglected to report any provisions. Of the three networks, NBC failed to report or adequately define the provisions in six of 13 stories (46.2 percent); ABC did not in 10 of 18 stories (55.6 percent); and CBS was remiss in nine of 15 stories (60.0 percent).

OVERALL COVERAGE. When researchers evaluated the comprehensiveness of the overall defense-budget coverage during the three-month period, they found that although it was more comprehensive than the COLA coverage, there was still much room for improvement.

Effects.

Researchers identified 25 major effects associated with the defense-spending proposals, again by closely monitoring the testimony of Congressional hearings and selected print-media coverage, and keeping a list of all effects mentioned. They were then categorized as follows:

On the Budget/Budget Deficit.

Discussion of:

1. the amount by which a proposal would reduce the deficit in FY 1986 or over a three-year period; of how much money a proposal would save;

2. a proposal's effect on other domestic programs in the budget;

3. a proposal as cutting the deficit far less than is necessary;

4. cuts as having no real impact; of "phantom" cuts from "unspecified" reforms;

5. the House budget package as cutting the deficit by about the same amount of money as the Senate budget package;

6. a proposal as cutting President Reagan's defense budget by more than he wanted; of Reagan having to accept deeper cuts;

7. a freeze proposal as still allowing outlays for FY 1986 to increase $15 to $20 billion over the FY 1985 level;

8. a freeze proposal as actually being a 4-percent real cut;

9. a freeze proposal as still allowing the FY 1986 level to be 50 percent ahead of 1980 in real-growth terms.

On the Economy.

Discussion of a proposal's effect on:

10. interest rates;

11. inflation;

12. tax increases;

13. economic growth;

14. health of the economy.

On Defense Programs/Defense of the Nation.

Discussion of a proposal as:

15. compromising the defense of the country;

16. not compromising the defense of the country;

17. hurting chances for arms reductions;

18. resulting in a dangerous deletion of weapons systems;

19. resulting in defense programs being extended and delayed;

20. resulting in the closing of military bases;

21. resulting in the Soviets increasing their weapons superiority;

22. resulting in reduced military pay and pensions;

23. resulting in the release of civilian employees from defense programs;

24. resulting in increased efficiency of the military; as stopping unneeded military build-up;

25. still allowing for new weapons systems; as not deleting weapons systems such as the B1 Bomber, the Trident Submarine, and the M1 Tank.

Of the 25 identified effects that could result if the defense-budget proposals were enacted, overall network coverage failed to address five of them. One-third of the coverage on effects--88 of 260 lines--was devoted to the effect that President Reagan would have to accept deeper cuts than he desired. (Again, lines were used instead of seconds for greater accuracy in determining amount of coverage.)

It is revealing to analyze the amount of coverage devoted to the different categories of defense effects. Defense effects were separated into three categories: "On the Budget/Budget Deficit," "On the Economy," and "On Defense Programs/Defense of the Nation." (However, when effects "On the Economy" were coded, coders could not determine whether they were Social Security or defense effects, since the impact was reported as the effect of an overall budget package, which included both Social Security and defense proposals. Thus, they were coded as effects of both subjects, and will not be discussed here to avoid repetition. For a discussion of this category, see page 16.)

The networks again were most interested in the effects of the various defense-spending proposals on the budget and the budget deficit. Of the 345 lines devoted to coverage of defense-spending effects, 214, or 62.0 percent, emphasized the effect of the proposals on the federal deficit. Of the nine specific effects identified in this category, the networks mentioned seven. The networks neglected to mention two effects: one that discussed the freeze proposal as a 4-percent real cut, and one that discussed the freeze proposal as allowing the 1986 funding level to be 50 percent ahead of 1980 in real-growth terms. The effect that received the largest percentage of coverage in this category, 88 of 214 lines (41.1 percent), regarded the amount of money the proposal would cut from President Reagan's defense budget.

Individually, the three networks followed a familiar pattern. ABC accounted for half of the coverage in the "budget/budget deficit" category--107 of 214 lines, and raised seven of the nine effects. CBS offered 79 lines (36.9 percent) and mentioned six effects, while NBC accounted for 28 lines (13.1 percent) and raised three effects.

The other category of defense-spending effects, "On Defense Programs/Defense of the Nation," received 91 lines, or 26.4 percent of the effects coverage. Of the 11 specific effects in this category, only one was not reported: the effect of a proposal on chances for arms reductions. The specific effect reported at least twice as much as the others discussed how a proposal would compromise the defense of the country.

In evaluating the individual networks' performance in this category, researchers found ABC's coverage the most comprehensive, with 56 of 91 lines (61.5 percent) and nine of 11 effects. NBC offered 20 lines (22.0 percent) and four effects, while CBS's coverage followed with 15 lines (16.5 percent) and three of 11 effects.

Terms Explained.

Network coverage of defense spending was poorer than COLA coverage in explaining or defining budgetary terms with complex or unclear meanings (e.g. the difference between "no growth" and "zero growth"), as Chart 9 demonstrates. During the viewing period, the words and terms identified by researchers in defense stories were used by the networks 36 times; 19 terms, or 52.8 percent, were not explained or defined by the networks. Thus, over one-half of unclear defense-budget terms went

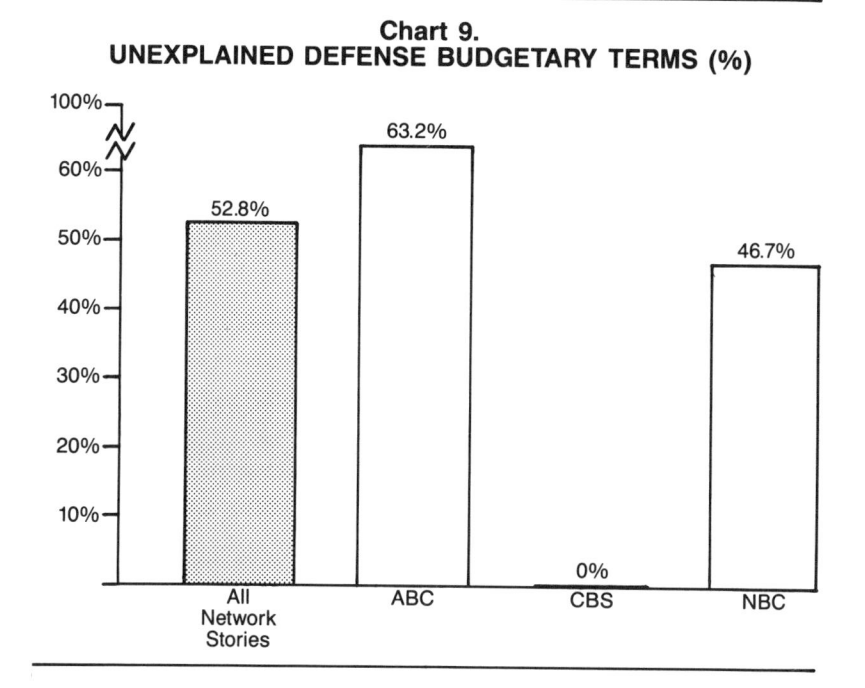

Chart 9.
UNEXPLAINED DEFENSE BUDGETARY TERMS (%)

	All Network Stories	ABC	CBS	NBC
%	52.8%	63.2%	0%	46.7%

unexplained, compared to less than one-third of unclear COLA-budget terms.

Individually, CBS explained the two unclear terms it used. NBC failed to explain seven of 15 terms (46.7 percent), while ABC left 12 of 19 terms unexplained (63.2 percent).

SUMMARY. In summary, analysis of the networks' coverage of defense spending suggests that coverage again was not comprehensive, regardless of whether it was measured by individual stories or overall coverage. If judged on a story-by-story basis, slightly over one-third of the stories met the minimum standard of comprehensiveness, and over one-half of the stories neglected to give or adequately define the basic provisions of the defense proposals. If judged by overall coverage over the three-month period, the networks' performance was still far below par. Again, they did not do a thorough job of covering the provisions and effects surrounding the defense proposals, and they neglected to define or explain unclear terms over one-half of the time.

Individually, NBC in general substantially outperformed ABC and CBS as measured by the study's criteria of comprehensiveness, although it devoted the least amount of coverage--213 lines.

Again, it is interesting to note that CBS deviated from the other two networks with regard to the amount of coverage devoted to defense spending. While CBS devoted a much larger percentage of its coverage to Social Security than did ABC and NBC, it also devoted much less of its coverage to defense spending. CBS used a total of 175 lines to report defense-budget issues, effects, and provisions, compared to 366 by ABC and 213 by NBC.

BALANCE

The issues surrounding the defense-spending

proposals also proved to be useful measures of balance, because they were either in support of or in opposition to increased defense spending. Researchers identified seven significant issues around which the defense-spending debate revolved. As with the Social Security issues, these were determined by analyzing all of the testimony presented in the Congressional hearings on defense spending, as well as examining selected print-media coverage of the debate. Researchers found that these seven issues were consistently discussed in the budget debate over defense spending.

The issues, and the viewpoints they supported, are listed below:

Issues in Opposition to Increased Defense Spending:

1. Controlling the deficit is the top priority.
2. The previous military build-up was successful.
3. The Pentagon suffers from a credibility gap.

Issues in Favor of Increased Defense Spending:
4. National security will be threatened if cuts are made.
5. The character of the defense budget is unique.
6. The defense budget sends a message to the Soviets.

Neutral Issues:

7. Reflection of cuts on President Reagan.

(Complete definitions of each issue can be found in the Appendix.)

Again, to evaluate the balance of coverage on this polarized topic, researchers measured the amount of coverage (in lines) given to issues supporting and opposing increased defense spending.

The pattern of imbalance found in COLA coverage persisted when coverage of defense spending was analyzed, as network coverage again was imbalanced in favor of a particular viewpoint. Coverage largely opposed an increase in defense spending by over a two-to-one margin. As Chart 10 demonstrates, the networks devoted 192 lines, or 65.5 percent, to issues opposed to increased spending. In contrast, they devoted 91 lines, or 31.1 percent, to issues in favor of more defense spending. Neutral issues received 10 lines, or 3.4 percent of the issues coverage.

Chart 11 shows the amount of coverage given to each individual issue. Over three-quarters of the coverage (77.7 percent) was devoted to three issues: two opposed to increased defense spending, and one in favor. The issues dealing with the priority of controlling the deficit and the Penta-

Chart 10.
COVERAGE DEVOTED TO ISSUES FAVORING AND OPPOSING INCREASED DEFENSE SPENDING (%)

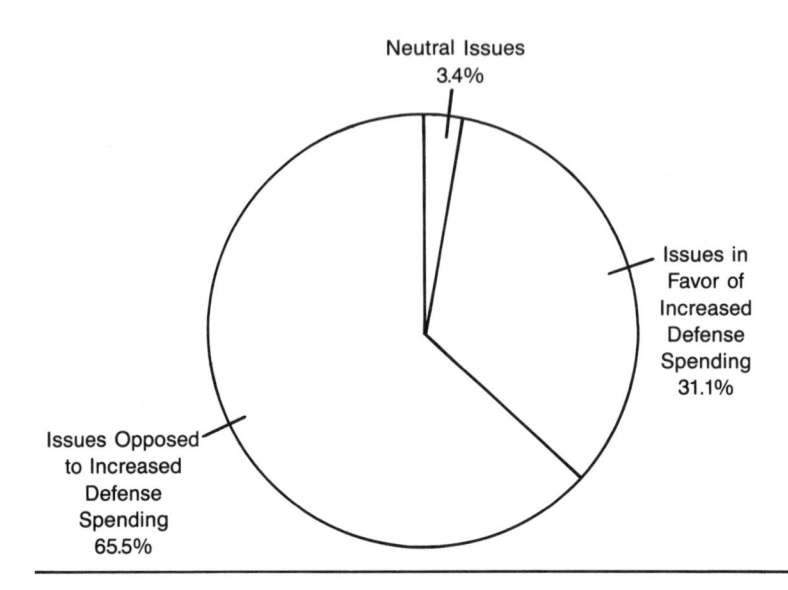

Neutral Issues 3.4%

Issues in Favor of Increased Defense Spending 31.1%

Issues Opposed to Increased Defense Spending 65.5%

gon's credibility gap received 89 and 75 lines of coverage, or 30.3 percent and 25.6 percent of coverage, respectively. The only issue of the three in favor of more money for defense was the national-security issue, to which 64 lines (21.8 percent of the issues coverage) were devoted. The remaining four issues each received 9.6 percent of the coverage or less.

Unlike COLA coverage, the individual networks' coverage did not necessarily mimic the overall network pattern. As Chart 12 illustrates, only ABC and NBC devoted more time to issues against increased defense spending. At first glance CBS's coverage appeared to be the most balanced of the three networks, since it presented a more balanced mix of opposing viewpoints. In fact, CBS was the only network to devote more coverage to issues in favor of increased spending, 51.0 percent to 43.1 percent. Neutral issues received 5.9 percent of the CBS coverage. However, CBS devoted a total of

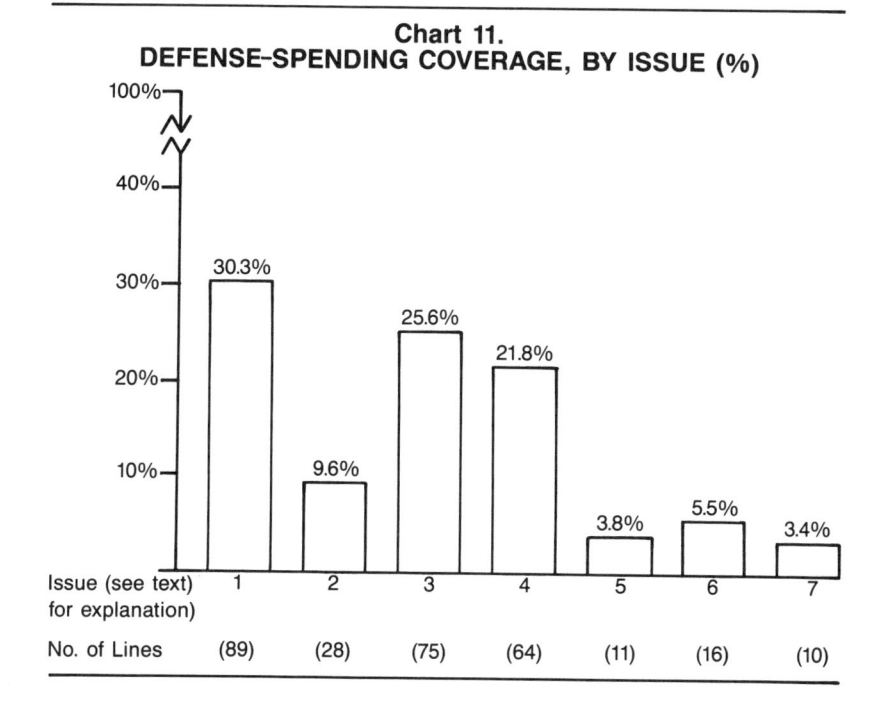

Chart 11.
DEFENSE-SPENDING COVERAGE, BY ISSUE (%)

Issue (see text for explanation)	1	2	3	4	5	6	7
Percent	30.3%	9.6%	25.6%	21.8%	3.8%	5.5%	3.4%
No. of Lines	(89)	(28)	(75)	(64)	(11)	(16)	(10)

only 51 lines to defense issues, whereas ABC and NBC offered 119 and 123 lines, respectively. CBS neglected to raise two of the defense issues, and was the only network that did not discuss the message that defense cuts would send to the Soviets.

NBC was again the least balanced of the networks in its coverage of the issues surrounding the defense-spending debate. Of its total coverage of defense issues, 76.4 percent of NBC's coverage was opposed to increased defense spending, compared to 17.9 percent in favor, and 5.7 percent neutral. Although the least balanced of the three networks, NBC addressed all seven issues, and was the only network to address the issue of whether the previous military build-up had been adequate.

ABC's coverage was opposed to increases in the defense budget by a margin of 63.9 percent to 36.1 percent. ABC raised four of the seven defense issues, and was the only network that failed to

Chart 12.
COVERAGE DEVOTED TO ISSUES FAVORING AND OPPOSING INCREASED DEFENSE SPENDING, BY NETWORK (%)

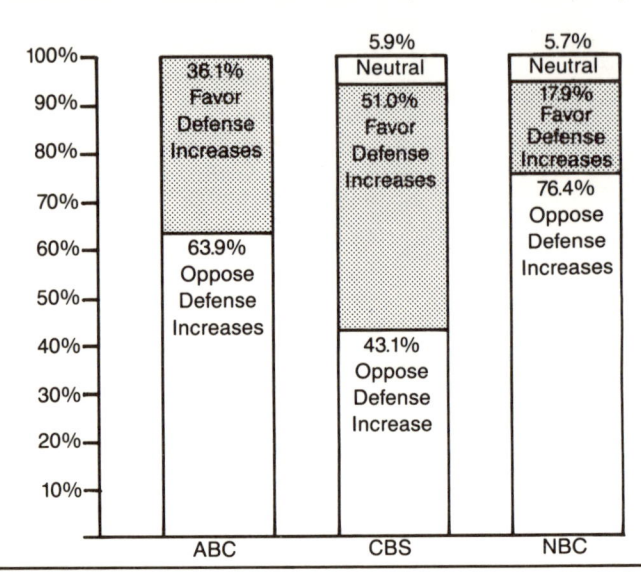

Network	Favor Defense Increases	Neutral	Oppose Defense Increases
ABC	36.1%	—	63.9%
CBS	51.0%	5.9%	43.1%
NBC	17.9%	5.7%	76.4%

discuss whether the unique character of the defense budget should determine how much money it is allocated, and whether President Reagan's image was tarnished by the cuts.

In summary, coverage of the defense-spending issues (with the exception of CBS) was, in terms of viewpoints presented, markedly opposed to increased spending levels, and thus substantially imbalanced.

CONCLUSION.

If the average viewer relied on the networks as the sole source of information on the defense-spending debate during the three-month period, he or she would have an incomplete and superficial understanding of the various effects and provisions involved in the different defense-budget proposals. The average network viewer also would have perceived the defense-spending debate as basically revolving around only three disputed issues: the priority of controlling the deficit, the credibility of the Pentagon, and the security of the country; in actuality four other important issues were also involved. As in the COLA coverage, the average network viewer's perspective on the defense-spending debate would be significantly limited.

IV. Survey Research

In addition to the content analysis of network coverage, researchers used survey research to assess people's positions with regard to Social Security cost-of-living allowances and defense spending, and their perceptions of the networks' coverage of the same issues. It should be noted that the findings of the survey research are by no means decisive, and, if used alone, would allow few claims of any significance. However, when used in conjunction with the content analysis, the survey research serves as a check on the accuracy of the content-analysis findings on balance of coverage.

METHODOLOGY

The survey was executed by Dr. Thomas R. Donohue of Boston University. It included 798 people who responded to a telephone questionnaire which solicited their views on Social Security COLAs and defense spending, and how they felt the networks covered those issues.

The sample was drawn from the top 100 media markets in the United States, with each market represented proportionate to its actual population in the United States. To be included in the sample, participants had to: watch network news more than once a week; be able to receive more than one television station in a primary (50-mile) signal area; and reside outside of remote areas.

The margin of error for the survey, with a sample of 798 people, is ±4 percent.

SOCIAL SECURITY

When respondents were asked whether they thought Social Security COLAs should be frozen or continue automatically in the coming year, a significant majority--82.5 percent--felt that COLAs should continue. Only 12.2 percent of the sample thought that the COLAs should be frozen, and 5.1 percent were unsure. Yet when asked whether they perceived network coverage as tending to favor freezing or continuing the COLAs, the majority of the sample, 52.4 percent, was not sure. Researchers were unable to determine whether viewers who responded "not sure" simply did not know if coverage favored a particular viewpoint, or thought the networks presented both sides objectively. There-

Chart 13.
SOCIAL SECURITY
44.8% of respondents had an opinion on whether network coverage favored a particular viewpoint.
Of those respondents:

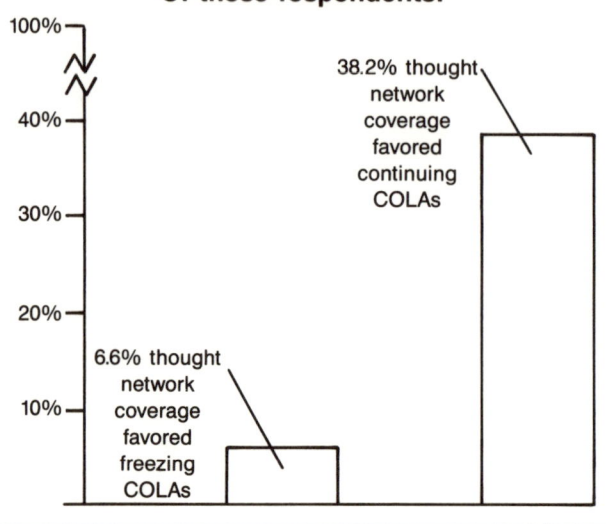

- 6.6% thought network coverage favored freezing COLAs
- 38.2% thought network coverage favored continuing COLAs

Chart 14.
SOCIAL SECURITY
**12.2% of respondents felt that COLAs should be frozen.
Of those respondents:**

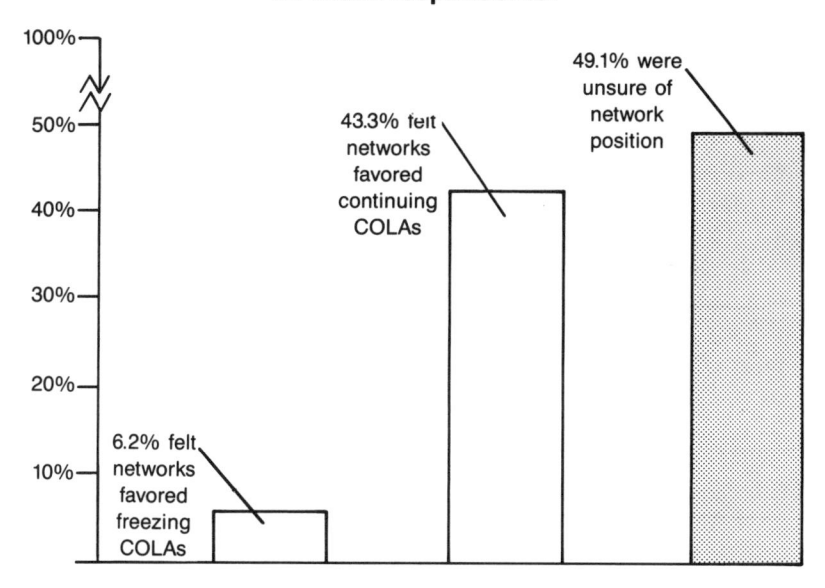

- 6.2% felt networks favored freezing COLAs
- 43.3% felt networks favored continuing COLAs
- 49.1% were unsure of network position

**82.5% of respondents felt that COLAs should continue.
Of those respondents:**

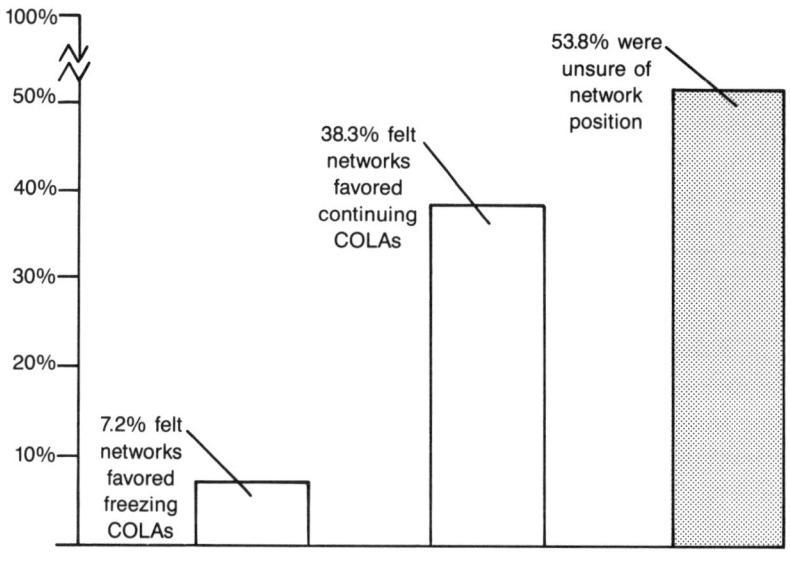

- 7.2% felt networks favored freezing COLAs
- 38.3% felt networks favored continuing COLAs
- 53.8% were unsure of network position

fore, researchers analyzed only the responses of people with definite opinions on the topic.

As Chart 13 demonstrates, of the people who did have an opinion, only 6.6 percent thought network coverage favored freezing the COLAs, whereas 38.2 percent felt the networks were in favor of continuing the COLAs. Thus, by a margin of almost six to one, respondents felt that network coverage of Social Security was in favor of continuing, rather than freezing, cost-of-living allowances. These findings seem to corroborate the content-analysis findings on the imbalance of network coverage of the COLAs; at the very least, they are not contradictory.

In conducting a series of cross-tabulations of responses, researchers found an interesting trend in the relationship between the respondents' position on COLAs and their perceptions of the networks' position on the same issue. Chart 14 illustrates that of the 97 people who felt that COLAs should be frozen, only 6.2 percent thought that network coverage reflected their opinion, while 43.3 percent felt coverage favored continuing the COLAs (49.1 percent were not sure). Of the 658 people who felt that COLAs should continue, 7.2 percent thought the networks favored freezing the COLAs, while 38.3 percent felt the coverage reflected their view; 53.8 percent were unsure. This lends credence to the findings of the content analysis--that network coverage was imbalanced in its opposition to a COLA freeze.

DEFENSE

People's opinions on defense spending were not as polarized as they were on COLAs. When respondents were asked whether they were in favor of increasing government spending on military and defense programs, 18.7 percent felt that defense spending should be increased, 57.0 percent thought that it should be kept about the same, 10.9 percent thought that it should be reduced, and 13.2

percent were unsure. Again, when the respondents were asked whether they felt network coverage tended to favor increasing spending on defense, keeping it about the same, or reducing spending, the majority of the sample, or 47.4 percent, was unsure. (Researchers did not analyze the "not sure" answers because it was impossible to determine whether respondents did not know, or whether they thought coverage was balanced.)

As Chart 15 shows, of the people who felt strongly enough to form an opinion, only 7.1 percent thought coverage favored an increase in spending, while 44.3 percent thought coverage opposed an increase (28.3 percent felt it favored keeping spending about the same, and 16.0 percent thought it supported a reduction in spending). Thus, by a margin of over six to one, respondents felt that network coverage opposed, rather than supported, increases in defense spending. Again, these findings lend support to the content analy-

Chart 15.
DEFENSE SPENDING
51.4% of respondents had an opinion on whether network coverage favored a particular viewpoint.
Of those respondents:

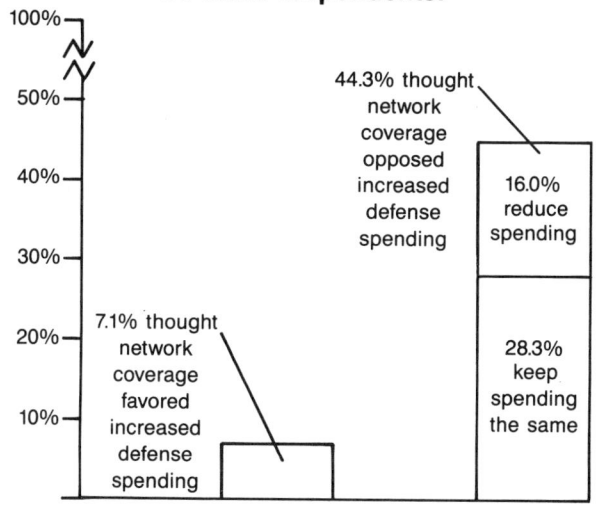

- 7.1% thought network coverage favored increased defense spending
- 44.3% thought network coverage opposed increased defense spending
- 16.0% reduce spending
- 28.3% keep spending the same

Chart 16.
DEFENSE SPENDING
18.7% of respondents felt that defense spending should be increased. Of those respondents:

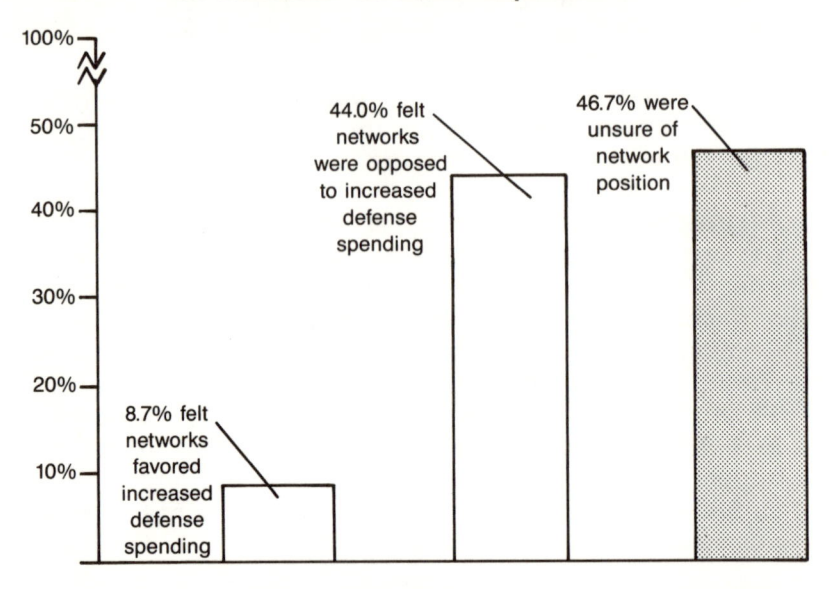

- 8.7% felt networks favored increased defense spending
- 44.0% felt networks were opposed to increased defense spending
- 46.7% were unsure of network position

67.9% of respondents were opposed to defense-spending increases. Of those respondents:

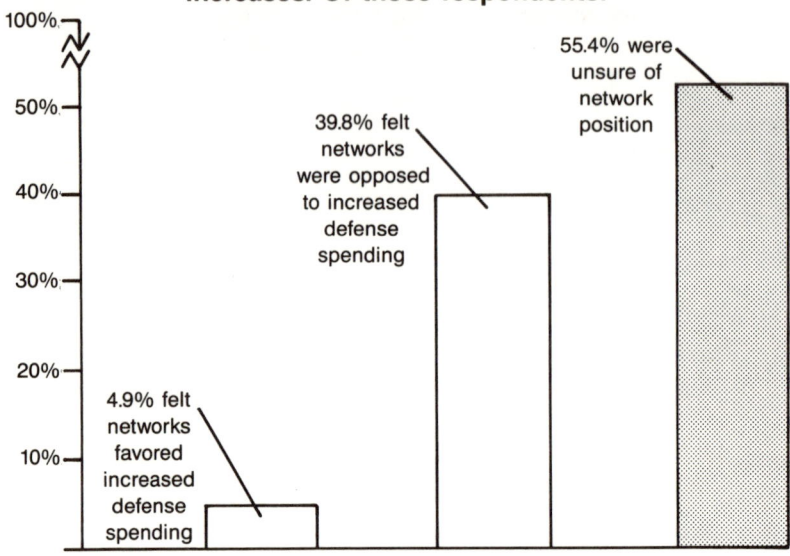

- 4.9% felt networks favored increased defense spending
- 39.8% felt networks were opposed to increased defense spending
- 55.4% were unsure of network position

sis regarding the networks' imbalanced coverage of defense spending.

When the cross-tabulations of responses were conducted, researchers again found a trend in the relationship between the respondents' position on defense spending and their perceptions of the networks' position on the same issue. According to Chart 16, of the 149 people who felt that defense spending should be increased, only 8.7 percent thought that network coverage reflected their opinion, while 44.0 percent felt coverage opposed the increase (46.7 percent were unsure). Of the 542 people who were against increases in defense spending, 4.9 percent thought the networks favored increased defense spending, while 39.8 percent felt the coverage mirrored their view; 55.4 percent were unsure. These findings again give credence to the validity of the content-analysis findings, which indicated that network coverage of defense spending was opposed to increases in defense spending, and was thus imbalanced.

V. Other Findings

The main objective of the study was to evaluate the comprehensiveness and balance of nightly news coverage on the budget debates over Social Security and defense spending. Yet the study also revealed some interesting findings on the networks' sources of information.

In measuring the "source" variable, coders recorded the amount of coverage (in lines) that various sources commanded. These sources were categorized as follows: experts/analysts; Congressmen; non-elected government officials; interest-group representatives; President Reagan; private citizens; journalists; others; and unattributed. (A full explanation of each category can be found in the Appendix.)

A frequently criticized characteristic of broadcast coverage has been its overreliance on government sources, to the exclusion of others.* As with most legislative matters, however, government figures were principal players in the debates over Social Security COLAs and defense spending, and thus were prime sources for comment on the various issues involved in the debates. When researchers

---

*See CNN vs. the Networks: Is More News Better News? (Washington, D.C.:The Media Institute, 1983); and Chemical Risks: Fears, Facts, and the Media (Washington, D.C.:The Media Institute, 1985).

aggregated the three categories of government sources (Congressmen, non-elected government officials, and President Reagan), government figures were sources of information for almost one-half (49.5 percent) of the Social Security issues, and for nearly two-thirds (63.5 percent) of the defense issues.

However, because each category of government source has its own vested interests (<u>e.g.</u> Congress and the Administration are often at odds over various proposals), researchers also analyzed the three governmental-source categories separately. Using this method they found that, contrary to their expectations, the networks used journalists as sources more often than any single category of government figures for both Social Security and defense-spending issues.

SOURCES FOR SOCIAL SECURITY ISSUES

Whom did the networks use for explanation of, and enlightenment on, the issues involved in the COLA debate? As Chart 17 demonstrates, the networks used journalists most often as a source of information for Social Security issues. Statements about issues by either anchormen or reporters accounted for 31.6 percent of the network coverage devoted to issues.

Congressmen were close behind as the second most popular source of information, accounting for 29.0 percent of the coverage. President Reagan captured 12.1 percent of the coverage, while private citizens, or "man-in-the-street" types, accounted for 10.9 percent. The remaining four categories each received less than 10 percent of the issues coverage, and commanded only 16.4 percent of the coverage when combined. Of special interest: Outside experts or analysts, who presumably would have been quite conversant with the issues surrounding the various budget proposals, were never consulted by the networks.

Chart 18 illustrates the percentages of coverage

various sources commanded on the individual networks. ABC deviated from the overall network pattern, and relied overwhelmingly on Congressmen as the main source of information for Social Security issues. They accounted for 45.5 percent of ABC's issues coverage. Receiving 16.1 percent each of the ABC coverage were journalists and President Reagan. Non-elected government officials were close behind with 13.4 percent of the coverage, followed by interest-group representatives with 8.9 percent.

CBS, in contrast, used journalists as its primary source of information for COLA issues; they received 41.9 percent of the coverage. Congressmen commanded 22.9 percent of the coverage, while private citizens followed with 12.3 percent. The remaining three categories of sources were not considered very significant, as each received less than 10 percent of the issues coverage.

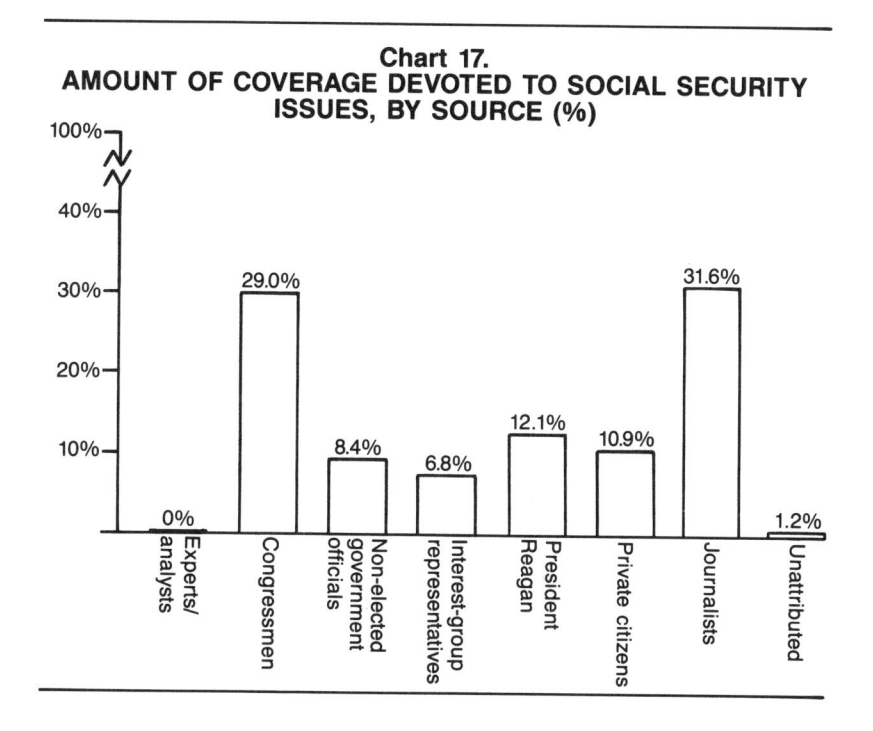

Chart 17.
AMOUNT OF COVERAGE DEVOTED TO SOCIAL SECURITY ISSUES, BY SOURCE (%)

Source	Percent
Experts/analysts	0%
Congressmen	29.0%
Non-elected government officials	8.4%
Interest-group representatives	6.8%
President Reagan	12.1%
Private citizens	10.9%
Journalists	31.6%
Unattributed	1.2%

Chart 18.
SOURCES USED FOR SOCIAL SECURITY ISSUES, BY NETWORK (%)

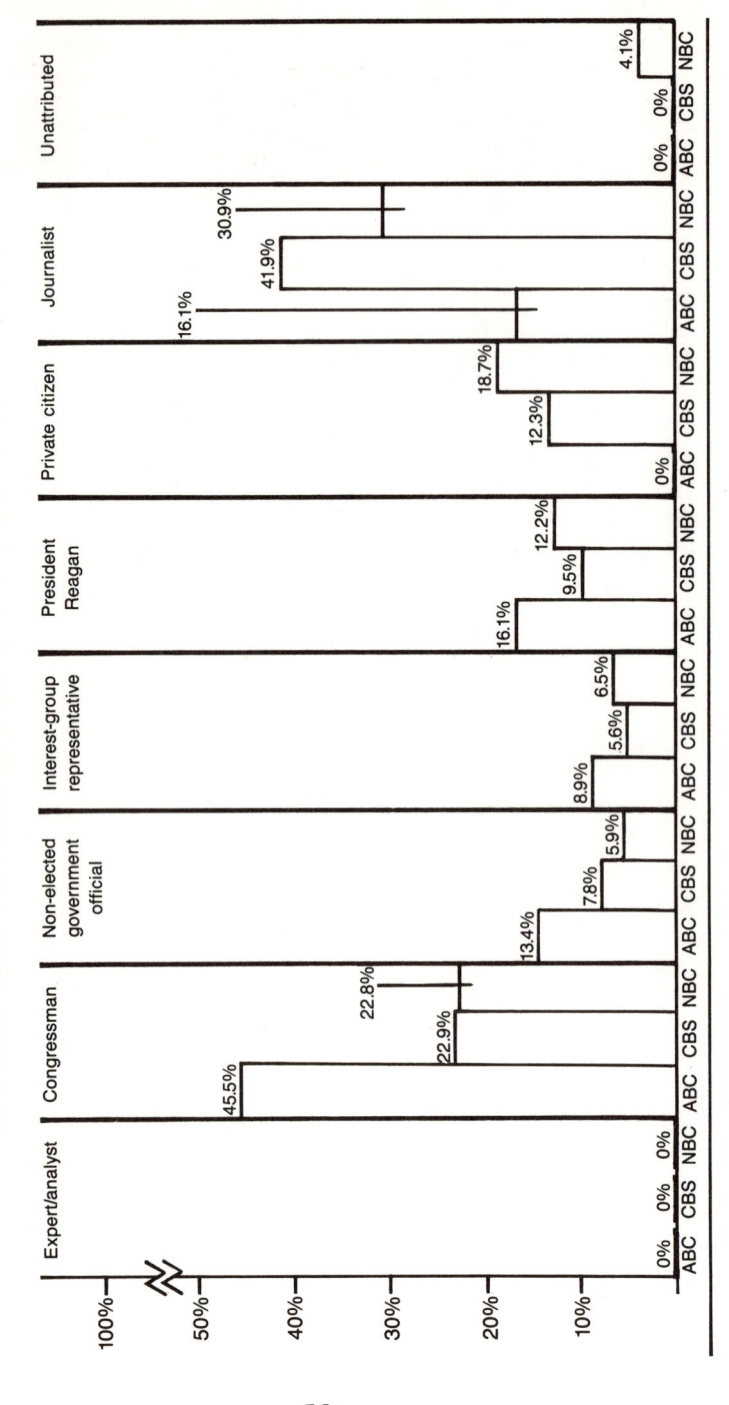

Source	ABC	CBS	NBC
Expert/analyst	0%	0%	0%
Congressman	45.5%	22.9%	22.8%
Non-elected government official	13.4%	7.8%	5.9%
Interest-group representative	8.9%	5.6%	6.5%
President Reagan	16.1%	9.5%	12.2%
Private citizen	0%	12.3%	18.7%
Journalist	16.1%	41.9%	30.9%
Unattributed	0%	0%	4.1%

NBC used journalists as sources of information for 30.9 percent of its issues coverage, and Congressmen for 22.8 percent. Unlike the other two networks, however, NBC relied substantially more on private citizens or "men-in-the-street" as sources of information--they accounted for 18.7 percent of NBC's issues coverage. President Reagan received 12.2 percent of the coverage, while non-elected government officials, interest-group representatives, and unattributed sources each received 6.5 percent or less of the issues coverage. Experts/analysts received no coverage.

These findings demonstrate that network coverage, by a substantial amount, relied on journalists and Congressmen as the two primary sources of information on the issues involved in the Social Security budget debate.

SOURCES FOR DEFENSE ISSUES

As with Social Security issues, the networks used journalists most often as the source of information on defense-spending issues. Chart 19 illustrates that comments on defense issues by reporters and anchormen commanded 27.0 percent of the networks' issues coverage.

However, non-elected government officials, rather than Congressmen, were the second most-used source of information on defense issues, capturing 24.2 percent of the coverage. Congressmen and President Reagan accounted for nearly the same amount of coverage, receiving 19.8 percent and 19.5 percent of the coverage, respectively. The networks were not very interested in the comments of outside experts/analysts, whose comments comprised only 3.1 percent of the total issues coverage; interest-group representatives and private citizens were not consulted at all.

Chart 20 shows the percentages of coverage devoted to various sources on each of the three networks. Unlike the pattern that emerged in the Social Security coverage, several major differences were observed among the networks in defense issues. ABC again deviated from the overall network pattern and relied on President Reagan, rather than journalists, as the primary source of information; he accounted for 28.6 percent of ABC's issues coverage. After President Reagan, ABC turned to Congressmen, journalists, and non-elected government officials about equally; they commanded 21.0 percent, 20.2 percent, and 19.3 percent of the issues coverage respectively. Although ABC devoted only 7.6 percent of its issues coverage to outside experts/analysts, it was the only network to consult them at all.

Unlike ABC, CBS used Congressmen most often as its source for defense-spending issues, accounting for 37.3 percent of the issues coverage on CBS. President Reagan was a close second, however, receiving 33.3 percent of the coverage. Surprisingly, and contrary to the overall network pattern, CBS used journalists relatively little as a

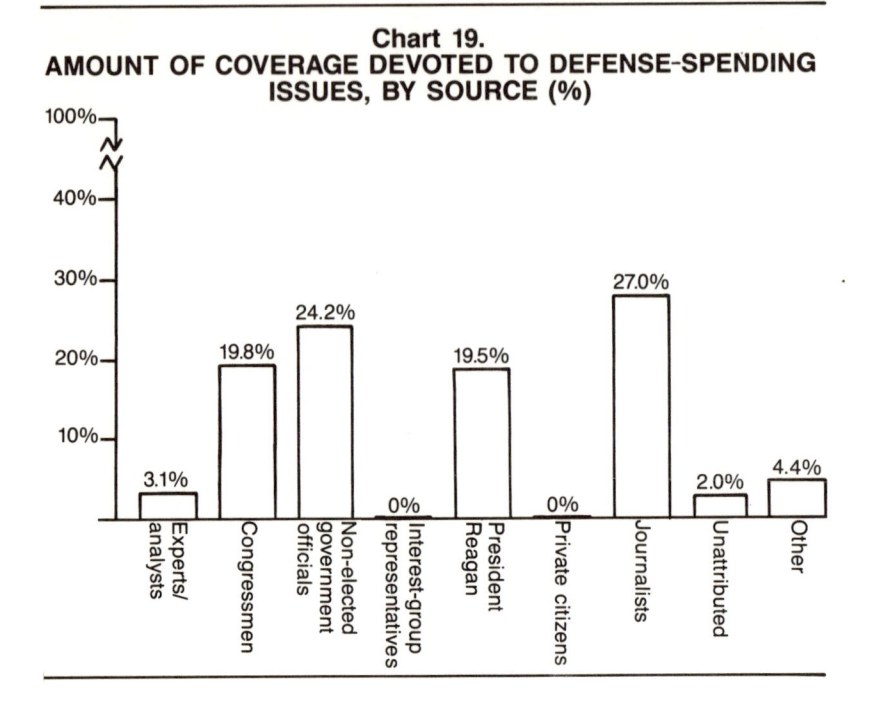

Chart 19.
AMOUNT OF COVERAGE DEVOTED TO DEFENSE-SPENDING ISSUES, BY SOURCE (%)

Source	%
Experts/analysts	3.1%
Congressmen	19.8%
Non-elected government officials	24.2%
Interest-group representatives	0%
President Reagan	19.5%
Private citizens	0%
Journalists	27.0%
Unattributed	2.0%
Other	4.4%

Chart 20.
SOURCES USED FOR DEFENSE-SPENDING ISSUES, BY NETWORK (%)

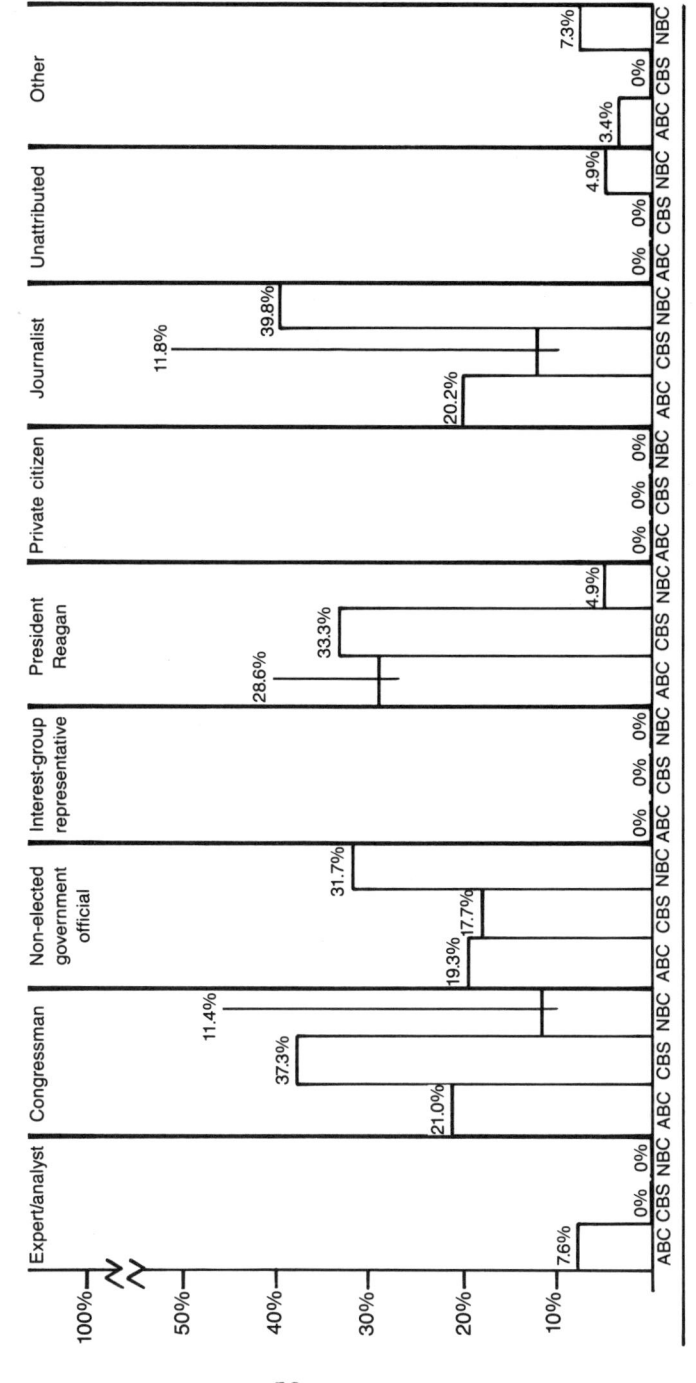

source of information on defense issues; their statements accounted for 11.8 percent of the coverage.

NBC followed the overall network pattern, using journalists as sources of information for 39.8 percent of its issues coverage, and non-elected government officials for 31.7 percent. Unlike ABC and CBS, however, NBC relied significantly less on Congressmen and President Reagan. These two categories accounted for only 11.4 percent and 4.9 percent respectively of NBC's issues coverage, far below the other two networks.

Unlike the Social Security coverage, no consensus emerged among the networks as to the most frequently quoted source of information for defense issues. However, journalists and government figures (Congressmen, non-elected government officials, and President Reagan) were still consulted a majority of the time, to the virtual exclusion of outside experts/analysts and others.

VI. Appendix

I. <u>Words and Terms</u>

Below is a list of words and terms associated with the budget that require further explanation before the uninitiated, or average, viewer can fully understand their meaning:

Budget Authority
Constant Dollars
Consumer Price Index (CPI)
Cost-of-Living Allowance (COLA)
Entitlement Programs
Freeze
Indexing
Means Test
Means-Tested Programs
No Growth
Nominal Freeze
Outlays
Real Cut
Real Freeze
Real Growth
Revenue Sharing
Spending Authority
Supplemental Security Income (SSI)
Supply-Side Economics
Zero Growth

II. Provisions of Proposals

For this study, a provision was defined as a written, formal statement of a condition; a stipulation or qualification; a portion of a Congressional bill or act; or a requisite action upon which rests the effectiveness of the proposal. Below is a list of the basic provisions associated with the Social Security COLA and defense-spending proposals:

A. Social Security COLAs

1. Eliminates funding for COLAs in Fiscal Year (FY) 1986; full funding for COLAs in FY 1987 and 1988; adds $1.3 billion over three years for Supplemental Security Income (SSI).

2. Provides 2-percent funding for COLAs in FY 1986, as long as inflation stays at 4 percent or below.

3. Provides full funding for COLAs in FY 1986, 1987, and 1988.

B. Defense Spending

1. Freezes budget authority at FY 1985 level for FY 1986; inflation-rate increase plus 3 percent in FY 1987 and 1988.

2. Provides inflation-rate increase in budget authority for FY 1986; inflation-rate increase plus 3 percent in FY 1987 and 1988.

3. Provides inflation-rate increase plus 3 percent in FY 1986.

4. Provides inflation-rate increase plus 6 percent in FY 1986.

5. Provides inflation-rate increase plus 8 percent in FY 1986.

III. Effect of Proposals

For this study an effect was defined as a discernible impact or change that would result if a particular proposal were implemented/not implemented; a resultant condition of a proposal. Effects were divided into four categories: On the Budget/Budget Deficit; On the Economy; On Individuals; and On Defense Programs/Defense of the Nation. Below is a list of the effects, divided by category, associated with the Social Security COLA and defense-spending proposals:

SOCIAL SECURITY COLAs

A. On the Budget/Budget Deficit.

Discussion of:

1. the amount by which a proposal would reduce the deficit in FY 1986 or over a three-year period; of how much money a proposal would save;

2. a proposal's effect on other domestic programs in the budget;

3. a proposal as cutting the deficit far less than is necessary;

4. cuts as having no real impact; of "phantom" cuts from "unspecified" reforms;

5. the House budget package as cutting the deficit by about the same amount of money as the Senate budget package.

B. On the Economy.

Discussion of a proposal's effect on:

6. interest rates;

7. inflation;

8. tax increases;

9. economic growth;

10. health of the economy.

C. On Individuals.

Discussion of:

11. a proposal's effect on people with incomes greater than the official poverty line;

12. a proposal's effect on the approximately 3.3 million poor households that would experience losses of benefits averaging $10 to $15 per month;

13. a proposal's effect on the average retired worker's or couple's benefits over three years;

14. a proposal's effect on the average recipient's benefits over the course of a lifetime;

15. a proposal's effect on the ability of the elderly to pay for energy, food, visits to the doctor, busfare, etc.;

16. a proposal's effect on Supplemental Security Income (SSI) benefits to individuals;

17. COLA freeze proposal's effect on the average citizen's benefits for one month or one year;

18. COLA freeze proposal as causing between 280,000 and 570,000 elderly people to drop

below the poverty line;

19. the effect of a two-percentage-point cut in COLAs on the average recipient's benefits over three years;

20. the effect of a two-percentage-point cut in COLAs on the average recipient for one month.

DEFENSE SPENDING

A. On the Budget/Budget Deficit.

Discussion of:

1. the amount by which a proposal would reduce the deficit in FY 1986 or over a three-year period; of how much money a proposal would save;

2. a proposal's effect on other domestic programs in the budget;

3. a proposal as cutting the deficit far less than is necessary;

4. cuts as having no real impact; of "phantom" cuts from "unspecified" reforms;

5. the House budget package as cutting the deficit by about the same amount of money as the Senate budget package;

6. a proposal as cutting President Reagan's defense budget by more than he wanted; as Reagan having to accept deeper cuts;

7. a freeze proposal as still allowing outlays for FY 1986 to increase $15 to $20 billion over the FY 1985 level;

8. a freeze proposal as actually being a 4-percent real cut;

9. a freeze proposal as still allowing the FY 1986 level to be 50 percent ahead of 1980 in real-growth terms.

B. On the Economy.

Discussion of a proposal's effect on:

10. interest rates;

11. inflation;

12. tax increases;

13. economic growth;

14. health of the economy.

C. On Defense Programs/Defense of the Nation.

Discussion of a proposal as:

15. compromising the defense of the country;

16. not compromising the defense of the country;

17. hurting chances for arms reductions;

18. resulting in a dangerous deletion of weapons systems;

19. resulting in defense programs being extended and delayed;

20. resulting in the closing of military bases;

21. resulting in the Soviets increasing their

weapons superiority;

22. resulting in reduced military pay and pensions;

23. resulting in the release of civilian employees from defense programs;

24. resulting in increased efficiency of tne military; as stopping unneeded military build-up;

25. still allowing for new weapons systems, as not deleting weapons systems such as the B1 Bomber, the Trident Submarine, and the M1 Tank.

IV. Issues Surrounding Proposals

For this study an issue was defined as a point of discussion, debate, or dispute surrounding the various budget proposals; or as a principle involved in discussion which involved value judgments. Below is a list of the issues associated with the Social Security COLA and defense-spending proposals:

A. SOCIAL SECURITY COLA ISSUES

1. Controlling the deficit is the top priority: discussion of whether the deficit can be reduced significantly without affecting Social Security, since Social Security is such a large part of the federal budget (20 percent); of whether cutting COLAs is the tough step needed to initiate other difficult cuts; of making necessary cuts as courageous.

2. The elderly are fairly well-off: discussion of whether the elderly are any poorer than the rest of the population in terms of accumulated wealth; of whether poverty rates for the elderly are lower than those for the rest of the population.

3. The overall package of cuts spreads the effects over the majority of the population: discussion of the advantages of spreading the effects of cuts across the population instead of on small groups of recipients; of whether Social Security recipients should share in the general sacrifice along with many other groups which are taking cuts (i.e. education, welfare, students, farmers, small business, etc.).

4. A freeze would result in the neglect of the poor and elderly: discussion of whether the welfare of the poor and elderly is being

disregarded; of whether President Reagan would prefer to sacrifice the welfare of the elderly in favor of weapons systems; of whether the welfare programs or "safety nets" to support the poor are declining.

5. <u>The elderly are being asked to bear a disproportionate amount of cuts</u>: discussion of whether the elderly have already paid their fair share; of whether the elderly already have had delays in benefits tantamount to reductions; of whether Social Security beneficiaries are being "raided."

6. <u>Social Security represents a contract/promise that cannot be broken</u>: discussion of whether President Reagan broke his campaign promise not to touch Social Security; of whether tampering with Social Security is akin to political suicide; of whether Social Security is still considered a "sacred cow;" of whether cuts would undermine the entire structure of retirement-income policy.

7. <u>Social Security adds nothing to the deficit</u>: discussion of how the Social Security program affects the federal deficit because it operates at a surplus and/or is organized as a separate trust fund; of whether it is legitimate to cut a self-contained program for general budgetary purposes.

8. <u>Larger issues of the Social Security system as a whole</u>: discussion of how the Social Security program will affect both young and old in the long run; of the merits and disadvantages of the system as a whole.

B. DEFENSE-SPENDING ISSUES

1. Controlling the deficit is the top priority: discussion of whether all interests, including defense, should have to bear the burden of budget cuts if any sizeable reductions are to be made; of whether cutting defense spending is the tough step needed to initiate other difficult cuts; of making necessary cuts as courageous.

2. The previous military build-up was successful: discussion of the Pentagon's build-up during the past four years as successful; of the Department of Defense (DOD) as the recipient of generous budget increases during the past four years; of whether DOD should be able to make do with defense spending (in constant dollars) that is higher than Vietnam war spending levels.

3. The Pentagon suffers from a credibility gap: discussion of the Pentagon's purchases of seemingly overpriced items (e.g. $1,500 pliers, $700 toilet seats) concurrent with its budget-increase requests; of whether the Pentagon is cost-conscious or cost-efficient; of whether the Pentagon has so much money that it cannot spend it all; of whether defense is no longer considered a "sacred cow;" of whether defense spending is now unpopular.

4. National security will be threatened if cuts are made: discussion of whether reductions in defense spending are a threat to national security.

5. The character of the defense budget is unique: discussion of whether the defense budget should be judged by the same criteria as other program budgets when it must take

into account contingencies that are unpredictable and/or beyond our control (<u>e.g.</u> wars, invasions, other countries' foreign policies).

6. <u>The defense budget sends a message to the Soviets</u>: discussion of whether cuts in defense spending would be the wrong message to send to the Soviets; of defense spending as a measure of U.S. political resolve.

7. <u>Reflection of cuts on President Reagan</u>: discussion of whether Reagan's image was affected when he broke his campaign promise not to compromise on defense-spending increases.

V. List of Issues as Categorized To Measure Balance

SOCIAL SECURITY COLAs

A. Issues in Favor of Freezing the COLA:

  1. Controlling the deficit is the top priority.

  2. The elderly are fairly well-off.

  3. The overall package of cuts spreads the effects over the majority of the population.

B. Issues Opposed to Freezing the COLA:

  4. A freeze would result in the neglect of the poor and elderly.

  5. The elderly are being asked to bear a disproportionate amount of cuts.

  6. Social Security represents a contract/promise that cannot be broken.

  7. Social Security adds nothing to the deficit.

C. Neutral Issues:

  8. Larger issues of the Social Security system as a whole.

DEFENSE SPENDING

A. Issues in Opposition to Increased Defense Spending:

  1. Controlling the deficit is the top priority.

2. The previous military build-up was successful.

   3. The Pentagon suffers from a credibility gap.

B. Issues in Favor of Increased Defense Spending:

   4. National security will be threatened if cuts are made.

   5. The character of the defense budget is unique.

   6. The defense budget sends a message to the Soviets.

C. Neutral Issues:

   7. Reflection of cuts on President Reagan.

VI. Sources Used in Coverage

Below is a list of the categories of sources who appeared or were cited in the network coverage of Social Security COLAs and defense spending:

1. <u>Expert/analyst</u>: Person with no affiliation (<u>i.e.</u> not identified with government, business, or interest group) who offers an "expert" opinion; someone from a university or think tank.

2. <u>Congressman</u>: U.S. Senator or member of the House of Representatives.

3. <u>Non-elected government official</u>: Administration official, <u>e.g.</u> a cabinet member or White House spokesperson; a federal-government employee serving by presidential appointment or having career (civil service) status.

4. <u>Interest-Group Representative</u>: Person serving or acting on behalf of a group whose members share a common interest, such as the American Association of Retired Persons, National Organization for Women, or AFL-CIO.

5. <u>President Reagan</u>: President of the United States.

6. <u>Private Citizen</u>: "Man-in-the-street" type; average citizen with no special affiliation.

7. <u>Journalist</u>: Anchorman or reporter for a network.

8. <u>Other</u>: Person who does not fit into any of the above categories.

9. <u>Unattributed</u>: Statements whose sources are not identified, <u>e.g.</u> "some people claim that...," "studies show...," etc.